I0820221

10 *Principles of* GODLY LEADERSHIP

Andrew Wommack

Published by Andrew Wommack Ministries, Inc.
Woodland Park, CO 80863

ISBN 13 HC: 978-1-66751-152-8
ISBN 13 eBook: 978-1-66751-153-5

For Worldwide Distribution, Printed in the USA

1 2 3 4 5 6 / 28 27 26 25

Contents

Introduction 1

Principle I Relationship with God

Chapter 1: Leaders Are Followers 5

Chapter 2: Prioritize God 11

Chapter 3: Love Others 17

Principle II Humility

Chapter 4: The Way Up Is Down 25

Chapter 5: Glory Belongs to God 31

Chapter 6: Let God Promote You 37

Principle III Character and Integrity

Chapter 7: You Have Influence 45

Chapter 8: Keep Your Promises 51

Chapter 9: Prepare Yourself 57

Principle IV Hear God's Voice

Chapter 10: The Good Shepherd 65

Chapter 11: Trust in the Lord 71

Chapter 12: Are You There? 77

Principle V Vision

Chapter 13: Get God's Plan 85

Chapter 14: Go Against the Flow 91

Chapter 15: Don't Limit God 97

Principle VI The Anointing

Chapter 16: Earn People's Respect 105

Chapter 17: Show Some Proof 111

Chapter 18: Release the Power 117

Principle VII Patience

Chapter 19: Wait on the Lord 125

Chapter 20: Gain Experience 131

Chapter 21: Keep Standing 137

Principle VIII Don't Quit

Chapter 22: Supernatural Strength 145

Chapter 23: Just Keep Going..................................... 151

Chapter 24: Press Toward the Mark 157

Principle IX Handling Persecution and Criticism

Chapter 25: You Will Face Resistance 165

Chapter 26: Get Rooted 171

Chapter 27: Take the High Road 177

Principle X Delegate Authority

Chapter 28: Don't Do It All 185

Chapter 29: They Will Be Sent 191

Chapter 30: Let Others Help You 197

Conclusion 203

Receive Jesus as Your Savior 205

Receive the Holy Spirit 207

Notes 209

Call for Prayer 211

About the Author 213

Introduction

Until recently, I had never been to a leadership conference or listened to any teaching about leadership. I'd just never pursued that subject before. And yet, at the time of this writing, I'm in a position where our ministry has more than 1,200 employees and about 8,000 students enrolled in our Charis Bible Colleges around the world.

Through our *Gospel Truth* daily television program and Gospel Truth Network, we have the potential to reach more than six billion people worldwide. We've put out millions of copies of our books, and they've been translated into dozens of languages.

Based on those statistics, I think I could say that I am a leader in the body of Christ. I'm not claiming to be more than I am. I know that there are many people God is using, but the Lord has put me in a position of leadership. And even though I would consider myself a leader, I've never really pursued it.

A few years ago, a man who is well known for teaching on leadership came to our Kingdom Business Summit at Charis Bible College in Woodland Park, Colorado. As he ministered and I sat and listened to him, I was just blessed by what he said. It was really good. I even took notes, which is not something I typically do.

One of the things that came out of that was I began thinking about how I became a leader without having pursued leadership training. It really kind of bothered me!

As I was praying about these things, the Lord began to speak to me. He showed me that what I've done over the years is just pursue Him. I simply looked to the Lord and sought a relationship with Him. Through our relationship, God has told me what to do and the steps to take. When I have conflict or there are problems in the ministry, I go to the Lord, He speaks to me, and those things get resolved. Really, my leadership has all come out of my relationship with God.

As you read through this book, you'll learn about 10 principles I believe are qualities of a truly godly leader. But the most important thing is having a personal relationship with God. The Lord will lead you into things like humility, integrity, hearing His voice, vision, anointing, patience, not quitting, handling criticism, and delegating authority through your relationship with Him.

Principle I

Relationship with God

Chapter 1

Leaders Are Followers

Be ye followers of me, even as I also am *of Christ.*

1 Corinthians 11:1

Many people try to learn about leadership by attending seminars, reading books, or listening to the experts. And while those may be good things, they're just self-help methods. The Apostle Paul, appointed by God as a leader to the Gentile churches, said, "Follow me as I follow Christ." So, godly leadership is really all about following. That's a totally different approach than most of the leadership teaching today.

The average teaching on leadership usually starts with how a person needs to have a vision. While I believe vision is important, it's not the first thing. Relationship with God is the first thing. Vision actually comes out of relationship with God.

To be a godly leader, your relationship with God must be more than what the average person has for one hour on Sundays. You can't just be part of the "nod-to-God" crowd. You've got to have a *living* relationship with the Lord. He has to be a part of your everyday life.

Unfortunately, most people who learn leadership principles will implement them independently of God. It's like they think, *If I just follow this person's formula and do steps X, Y, and Z, then I'll get their results*. But that's not the way it works.

I have a personal relationship with God. He has spoken to me and told me things that I need to know to fulfill the role of being a godly leader. For example, when it comes to dealing with a crisis or criticism, the Scripture tells me to cast all of my care on the Lord because He cares for me (1 Pet. 5:7). That's part of having a personal relationship with God—He cares for me!

At Charis Bible College, the predominant thing we teach about is having a relationship with God. We don't teach gimmicks, nor do we just teach steps or formulas. I'm not saying that there aren't steps and stages of your development as a leader, but we prioritize things. Everything really comes back to your personal relationship with God. That's where you begin.

I'm not against people who go to leadership conferences. But I'm saying that my life is not based on principles that I've learned from a conference or somebody's teaching. It has all come from my personal relationship with God.

If you are not drawing on your own relationship with God, then you can sit under the best leaders in the world, and learn all kinds of things, and I guarantee that you aren't going to be an effective and godly leader.

What's Inside of You?

I remember when I was in the sixth grade, I had a teacher who used a lot of practical things to illustrate the points he made. Once, he took a metal, one-gallon gas can and put it on a Bunsen burner. He heated that thing up to where it was nearly red hot. And then, he put the cap on it, took it off the burner, sat it on his desk, and just went on teaching.

I was sitting on the front row where I could see this teacher's desk up close. That meant this can was right in front of me. As the can cooled off, it began to crinkle and make popping noises. I watched that can get crushed right before my eyes. Eventually, it just bent in two, fell off the desk, and landed on the floor at my feet.

This teacher was illustrating that hot air occupies a higher volume than cold air. He heated that can and sealed it off so the surrounding atmospheric pressure couldn't get inside. That formed a partial vacuum inside of the can, and the pressure from the outside crushed it.

That was a lesson that I've never forgotten, and I've applied it throughout my life. I've watched many people try to cope and deal with the pressures that come against them. And what they're actually doing is trying to diminish all of the outside pressure on themselves.

They're trying to make everybody treat them a certain way and just adjust to their feelings. But they don't realize that their problems aren't because of pressure from the outside. The real problem is the vacuum that's on the inside of them. That's what is actually causing people to collapse.

It all comes back to having a relationship with God. If your relationship with the Lord is the way it's supposed to be, then you'll be able to stand against the criticism and pressure that comes your way because of Who is living on the inside of you (Gal. 2:20). You'll have enough security that you can delegate and let other people do things without being constantly worried. You'll be able to operate in faith. You'll be able to cast your care over on the Lord (1 Pet. 5:7).

You need to have the kind of relationship with God where you aren't just talking about Him. When you read the Bible, you shouldn't just read about what God did to somebody else. You need to be reading the Word with your heart and letting God speak to you. But that only happens when you're in communion with the Lord.

A Fragmented Life

> *For to be carnally minded* is *death; but to be spiritually minded* is *life and peace.*
>
> Romans 8:6

For many people, their lives are segmented or compartmentalized. Even some of those who are considered more spiritual only focus part of their life on God, while the rest is focused elsewhere. If they have devotional time, they may spend thirty minutes to an hour focusing on God, but then the rest of their day is totally carnal—they just live by whatever is pleasing to their flesh, just like the rest of the world. They don't keep their minds fixed on the Lord, and because of that, they don't live in perfect peace (Is. 26:3).

Many people will watch movies, read books, visit websites, and tell jokes that are contrary to living a godly lifestyle. They just view that as part of their secular life, separate from their spiritual life. They go to church on Sunday morning and depend on that to sustain them for the week. But for the rest of the time, they operate in gossip, anger, fear, and so many other things inconsistent with everything they heard in church.

My wife and I will occasionally watch movies, and it's really hard to find something good and wholesome. We'll be watching a movie that starts depicting things that are ungodly, and we have to turn it off. I just can't watch those kinds of things. I can't use those things for entertainment. And yet, there are people who can do that with no feelings of conviction whatsoever.

There are people who watch horror movies and harden their hearts by telling themselves, "It's just a movie; it's not real." The Bible says perfect love casts out fear (1 John 4:18). And the Apostle Paul wrote that God didn't give us a spirit of fear, but of power, love, and a sound mind (2 Tim. 1:7).

Why would you want to watch something that makes you anxious, condemned, fearful, and worried? Why watch something where there's just all kinds of immorality, cursing, and violence? Many people just end up living vicariously through the person on the screen, feeding their lust or unrighteous anger. That's carnal, and I don't believe that's the way God made us to be.

You don't just have a devotional part of your life where you pray for twenty to thirty minutes and then spend the rest of your day in strife, error, and ungodliness. As long as you're awake, you need to be in communion with the Lord.

Chapter 2

Prioritize God

Rejoice evermore. Pray without ceasing. In every thing give thanks: for this is the will of God in Christ Jesus concerning you.

1 Thessalonians 5:16–18

Each of us needs to have a personal relationship with the Lord where we "*pray without ceasing.*" I go walking a lot. On a typical day, I may walk over five miles in the morning. During those walks, I'll pray and commune with the Lord. But that's not the only time during my day that I do something like that.

If I'm driving, I'll listen to teaching or praise music, and I'll be worshiping God. I've even gotten to the point that when I'm sleeping, I'm dreaming about the things of the Lord. I am just trying to be in communion with Him.

When you prioritize your relationship with God, you will become someone He can use. He'll promote you in your job and at your church and do things in your life that He will want to replicate in the lives of others. If He can use you as an example to point people in the right direction, He will put you in leadership.

Everything that you need to know to be a godly leader will come out of your relationship with God. He will speak to you and tell you things like, "This isn't the right way to represent Me. You need to do this instead." He will show you the things you need to do. I can tell you that is true just from my own personal testimony.

Over the course of my life, I've made decisions that didn't look like they were very important at the time. They were just things that the Lord put on my heart. They came out of my relationship with Him. And when I followed God's leading, supernatural results happened.

I believe that unless you are a faithful follower of Jesus, you're going to make a poor leader. If you want to be a godly leader, you've got to make your relationship with God a priority. There are going to be a lot of demands placed upon you and your time. If you deviate from putting Jesus first and deal with all of these things on your own, Satan can use that to choke your leadership. You just won't be as effective.

It's like flying. A plane needs constant application of thrust and lift in order to fly. The moment you turn off the engines, that plane starts dropping. It may take a period of time before you hit the ground, but you've got to keep that power going if you want to stay in the air.

In a similar way, you've got to keep your relationship with God constant. Any time you let anything—the position that God has given you or even your ministry—take away from your personal relationship with God, you're cutting off the power. You're going to start sinking.

Servant to All

But he that is greatest among you shall be your servant.

Matthew 23:11

Christians should operate differently than the world. In the world system, people exercise dominion and authority in an ungodly way (Matt. 20:25 and Mark 10:42), but among believers, it shouldn't be so (Matt. 20:26–27 and Mark 10:43–44). The one who's going to be greatest must be servant of all.

Jesus illustrated this when He took off His outer garments, girded Himself with a towel, and went around washing His disciples' feet—a job that slaves did (John 13:4–16). And they were offended! Peter said, "*Thou shalt never wash my feet.*" But Jesus responded, "*If I wash thee not, thou hast no part with me*" (John 13:8). So, Peter eventually gave in and said, "*Not my feet only, but also* my *hands and* my *head*" (John 13:9).

Jesus served others. He said, "I'm the master, and yet here I am serving you. I'm giving you an example. This is the way it should be with other people" (John 13:13–15). This is because He was constantly in fellowship with His Father and put His Father's will first (Luke 22:42).

Next to Jesus, Joseph may be the greatest example of godly leadership in the Bible. When you read his story in Genesis, it looks like everything in his life was on a downward trajectory. God gave him dreams as a young man, where he was shown that he would be in a position of authority and his family would bow down to him (Gen. 37:5–11).

After that, Joseph's brothers threw him in a pit and sold him into slavery (Gen. 37:23–28). He was falsely accused by his master's wife and thrown into prison (Gen. 39:7–20). Even after he correctly interpreted the dreams of Pharaoh's butler and baker, he was forgotten for a time (Gen. 40:23). Despite all these things, Joseph held on to his relationship with God.

When the butler and baker were cast into prison, Joseph was charged with their care, and the Bible says, "*he served them*" (Gen. 40:4). That's amazing. There was Joseph, who could have been sitting there feeling sorry for himself after all the things that had happened to him, but he was serving others instead.

Joseph put his relationship with God first and became a servant of all. And because of that, when the butler remembered what Joseph had done for him, Joseph was called to interpret Pharaoh's dream. He went from prison to second in command of the most powerful nation on earth within a few hours' time (Gen. 41:9–45).

Christians are different, and we need to lead differently. There needs to be godly leaders—people who put their relationship with God ahead of everything else.

God Values You

In Revelation 2:1–3, Jesus tells John to write about the pastor of the Ephesian church, saying,

> *Unto the angel of the church of Ephesus write; These things saith he that holdeth the seven stars in his right hand, who walketh in the midst of the seven golden candlesticks; I know thy works, and thy labour, and thy patience, and how thou canst not bear them which are evil: and thou hast tried them which say they are apostles, and are not, and hast found them liars: and hast borne, and hast patience, and for my name's sake hast laboured, and hast not fainted.*

This is exceptional. Most of us would love to have this spoken by the Lord about our leadership. This pastor was a hard worker. He was laboring. He had dealt with errors. He was shepherding the people God gave him. Everything Jesus said here was good, but then He said in verses 4–5,

> *Nevertheless I have* somewhat *against thee, because thou hast left thy first love. Remember therefore from whence thou art fallen, and repent, and do the first works; or else I will come unto thee quickly, and will remove thy candlestick out of his place, except thou repent.*

Here was a man who was doing all of these good things at Ephesus, but Jesus was telling him, "You may be straight as a gun barrel, but you're twice as empty." Jesus was telling this pastor that he didn't have a strong personal relationship with God.

"*Thou hast left thy first love*," Jesus said. And if this man didn't repent, even though he was doing a lot of good things, Jesus was going to take that candlestick away. In the first chapter of Revelation, we learn that the word "candlestick" was talking about church. In other words, the Lord was going to lead those people someplace else.

You see, the Lord is more concerned about us and our personal relationship with Him than He is about what we do for Him. This is the foundation of the Christian life, and if you don't get the foundation right, anything you build on it is also going to be faulty (Matt. 7:24–27). It'll be susceptible to falling down and not lasting.

Relationship with God is not something you can bypass on your way to being a leader. In the world, most people are goal oriented. But if all your focus is on those goals, you'll be missing God.

Leadership is not about accomplishing things. You may be doing all kinds of good things, like the pastor at Ephesus, but if you are not grounded in a relationship with God, you will not be a godly leader. Whatever kingdom you are building outside of God's kingdom will not last.

Chapter 3

Love Others

For we must all appear before the judgment seat of Christ; that every one may receive the things done in his body, according to that he hath done, whether it be good or bad.

2 Corinthians 5:10

Someday, we're all going to stand before the Lord and answer to Him. Among other things, we will be answerable for how we lead. And there are a lot of people today who are leading in an ungodly way.

There are a lot of business leaders who have left a trail of bodies behind them, so to speak. They are just ruthless in how they deal with people. That's the way they got to a position of leadership, by using other people as steppingstones. But that's not a godly way of doing things.

The Lord has sent me many talented people over the years to help with this ministry. I could tell you story after story about the people who left what they were doing in the world to come and just serve, not promote themselves. It's been a blessing.

Years ago, there was one person who did a lot of good things for this ministry, and at the time, they were a godsend to us. They helped us establish a lot of good things. But at some point, I just had to tell this person it was time for them to leave.

You see, this person was just like a steamroller. If somebody got in their way, they were going to crush them. They would just run over a person. They left bodies—not physically damaged, but emotionally—all over the organization. And there were other people who they already had their sights set on. I just had to stop it.

When I finally told this person they had to go, they were shocked! They asked, "Is there some way that we can work this out?" And I responded, "If I thought that you even saw that what you were doing was wrong, we could work with that. But you think what you're doing is right."

That is not godly leadership. There is a big difference between the way the world teaches to lead by intimidation, command, and control, versus the way that God teaches us to lead.

Someone who has a relationship with God will think about the needs of others. If we would just put God first in our lives, all of our other priorities would fall into place, and we would be godly leaders.

Be Consistent

> *Remember them which have the rule over you, who have spoken unto you the word of God: whose faith follow, considering the end of* their *conversation. Jesus Christ the same yesterday, and to day, and for ever.*
>
> Hebrews 13:7–8

People often take that eighth verse out of context just to say that Jesus is the same yesterday, today, and forever—that He is unchanging in His love for us and other things. While that is true, if you put the verse back in its context, it is talking about leadership. It's saying that we shouldn't just follow people blindly.

You should follow someone as they follow Christ. Jesus is the same yesterday, today, and forever. Likewise, a godly leader should be consistent in their relationship with the Lord. They won't portray something on Sunday and then live differently Monday through Saturday.

Someone who is not following the Lord closely is going to have their leadership diminished. They are going to be susceptible to Satan drawing them away and getting them off track. It is just a tendency of fallen human beings. Every one of us has to deal with our flesh. And if we start to stray from what God has called us to do, He is going to correct us.

Consistency is one of the things in my life that has made a huge difference. I believe the Lord has put me in a position of leadership, not because I'm a great person, but because of my consistent personal relationship with Him.

One of the things that people often say about me is, "Andrew's the same." What they're saying is I act the same way all the time, whether I'm in front of an audience or I'm just talking with people in a casual setting. And when they say that, my first thought is, *Well, how does everybody else act?* It just seems weird to me that a person would act one way in front of the public and another way in private.

I've also been preaching the same things for decades. I may use different scriptures and add new stories as examples, but the foundational principles are the same. And I've tried to live out those things to the best of my knowledge. I've grown in my relationship with the Lord and become stronger in those things, but I haven't changed my direction. I just want to know God more and be closer to Him.

That's one of the reasons why I don't let my emotions get too high or too low. I'm just steady and consistent. I have emotions, but I've learned to harness them. I also don't worry about myself when I'm interacting with people, wondering, *What do they think about me?* But things weren't always that way.

Don't Look to Others

When I was younger, I was an introvert. I couldn't look a person in the face and talk to them. I was fine around friends and family, but talking to strangers petrified me.

One time, a man greeted me on the street and said, "Good morning." He was two blocks away and I was sitting in my car before I said, "Good morning," in response! I thought, *There must be something wrong with me!* It was because I was so timid and focused on what people would think of me.

When I first started ministering, I was so nervous and worried about what people would think of me that I would rush through my notes. It seemed like I would finish my whole sermon in five minutes! It was pitiful.

After one of my meetings, someone came up to me and said, "You've got some really good things to share. If you loved the people more than you love yourself, you could be a blessing." What this man said felt like a knife going into me, but he was right. I was only worried about what other people thought about me instead of thinking about them.

Most people would say I was just being timid or shy, but in fact, I was being self-centered. I didn't think I was better than everybody else, but I was so dependent on the acceptance of others that I was afraid I'd say or do something to make me look stupid. Really, that was just pride.

If you spell out the word pride, you'll see that "I" is at the center of it. In its simplest explanation, pride is just self-centeredness. It can manifest as thinking that you're better than everybody else. But if you think you're worse than everybody else, you're still self-centered. You're just constantly thinking about yourself and what people are going to think about you.

People who don't have a living relationship with the Lord are always going to look to others for their approval. That will only end in disappointment. And it will not make you a godly leader. I'll tell you, the only people who will let you down are the ones you lean on.

There have been times in my ministry where, outside of my wife Jamie, it seemed like the only one on my side was the Lord. I've been maligned and criticized, people have lied about me, and I've even been kidnapped. But I had a relationship with the Lord. He revealed Himself to me in a supernatural way, and I've never been the same since.

Principle II

Humility

Chapter 4

The Way Up Is Down

Likewise, ye younger, submit yourselves unto the elder. Yea, all of you *be subject one to another, and be clothed with humility: for God resisteth the proud, and giveth grace to the humble. Humble yourselves therefore under the mighty hand of God, that he may exalt you in due time.*

1 Peter 5:5–6

I got born again when I was eight years old, but by the time I was eighteen, I had become a religious Pharisee. I was taught that a person had to be holy to earn God's favor, so I lived as holy as anybody I knew.

I never used profanity when I spoke. I never smoked a cigarette. I never touched a drop of liquor. I didn't even drink coffee. You may be thinking, *Coffee?* Well, you have a scripture to stand on for drinking coffee. Mark 16:18 says, if believers "*drink any deadly thing, it shall not hurt them.*"

I don't say these things in a prideful way, but it just goes to show how religious I was. I did everything I could think of to please the Lord. I studied the Word. I never missed a church service. I even started special youth visitations where the teenagers in our church went around sharing the Gospel with people.

Those weren't bad things, but the problem was I was trusting in myself and thinking that I was better than other people. I was doing all of these extra things that other people weren't doing. And because of that, I thought that God owed me something.

Then, on March 23, 1968, I had a miraculous encounter with the Lord that totally changed my life. The Lord just showed up at a Saturday night prayer meeting, and I saw the glory of God. I didn't see it with my physical eyes; it came by revelation. And compared to the glory and holiness of God, all of my self-righteousness was like filthy rags (Is. 64:6).

Isaiah saw the glory of God and fell at His feet as if he was dead. He said, "*Woe* is *me! for I* am *undone; because I* am *a man of unclean lips*" (Is. 6:5). Here was a prophet of God who was living a relatively holy life compared to other people. But compared to God, he immediately recognized his unworthiness.

That night, instead of experiencing condemnation, I was overwhelmed by the supernatural love of God. I was drawn into a personal relationship with Him that wasn't based on what I could do, but rather on what Jesus had already done. And that produced humility in me.

I believe that if you make your relationship with the Lord the top priority in your life, He will produce humility in you. At some point, you will have to recognize that He is God, and you are not. You'll learn that the only way up in God's kingdom is down. And the Lord will keep you humble as long as you stay in fellowship with Him.

Complete Surrender

Saul of Tarsus was one of the most educated men of his day. He was considered a great leader in his community. But he wasn't living and leading in a godly way. He was leading through fear and intimidation, taking Christians and putting them to death or committing them to prison (Acts 9:1–2). But then the Lord showed up on the road to Damascus (Acts 9:3–4). Immediately, Saul said, "*Who art thou, Lord?*" (Acts 9:5). That's a pretty quick revelation!

Saul had been rejecting Jesus. He'd been doing things his own way. He was basically a god unto himself. He was determining who should live and who should die. But when Saul saw the glory of God, immediately, he humbled himself. After that, Saul of Tarsus became the Apostle Paul.

Paul evangelized much of the known world and wrote half of the books of the New Testament, and here we are, 2,000 years later, still talking about him. So, I think he qualifies as a godly leader. Humility isn't weakness, nor is it thinking poorly about yourself. It's having an understanding that God is God. He is Lord, and you are not. It's just submission to Him.

Years ago, there was a popular movie called *Chariots of Fire* which told the story of Eric Liddell. He was a British runner and committed Christian who competed in the 1924 Olympics. Liddell was scheduled to run the 100-meter dash on a Sunday. But because of his convictions, he refused to compete.

Back then, it was commonly accepted among Christians that Sunday was a special day set aside for worship, with shops closed and no sports. A lot has changed. How many people today would say, "No, I'm going to honor my God," and not compete in the biggest event of their lives?

Thankfully, he got another chance to race in the 400 meters. Right before the race, someone handed him a note that read, "*Them that honour me I will honour*" (1 Sam. 2:30). Then, he went out and won a gold medal, setting a world record in the process![1]

You may be thinking, *How is that leadership? He won a medal in an individual sport!* Well, Liddell went on to be a missionary to China. Then, when World War II broke out, he could have saved himself by using his notoriety. Instead, he spent the rest of his life serving others in a Japanese prison camp and was considered a leader by his fellow prisoners. Many people survived and owed their lives to Eric Liddell.

There are people who know what God has called them to do, and yet they are going to do it their own way. That's not a humble attitude. At the end of his life, when asked how he served God, it's said Liddell's last words were, "It's complete surrender."[2] He just lived his whole life honoring God. That's humility!

Seek First the Kingdom

> *But seek ye first the kingdom of God, and his righteousness; and all these things shall be added unto you.*
>
> Matthew 6:33

The things Jesus was talking about include what you eat, where you sleep, and what you're clothed with (Matt. 6:31)—your physical needs. A godly leader is a person who doesn't have their own agenda or seek after their own needs. They aren't promoting themselves. They just do what God tells them to do.

As I've submitted myself to God, I've learned to humble myself. If God tells me to do something, to the best of my ability I'm going to do it. Over the years, God has told me to do things that, in the natural, could not be done.

I used to be so poor I couldn't pay attention. Jamie and I even struggled to eat at times. When she was eight months pregnant, we once went for two weeks with nothing but water. There was no food whatsoever.

When some people say they are broke, they are talking about having $1,000 in the bank and needing to pay bills. When I tell you that we didn't have any money, I mean that we had nothing, zero, nada, zip! I would go out, pick up empty bottles, and return them just to have enough money to put gas in our car. Now, God has blessed our ministry with hundreds of millions of dollars' worth of assets. And I didn't intentionally seek property or money. All I did was seek God.

Years ago, when I was telling my mother (who was in her 90s by that time) about all the great things the Lord was doing through this ministry, she stuck her bony little finger in my face and said, "Andy, you know this is God." So, I replied, "Yes, ma'am, I know it's God." And then, she finished by saying, "You aren't smart enough to do all this!"

Some people may have been offended by something like that, but I knew exactly what my mother was talking about. If I was God, I wouldn't have picked me. But I knew that without God, I was like a zero with the rim knocked off. I humbled myself and put God first in my life. Because of that, the Lord was able to use me.

I haven't sought prosperity, but I've sought God, and prosperity came with the relationship. The things I've needed to fulfill the role God has given me have come because I've humbled myself and let Him provide.

Chapter 5

Glory Belongs to God

> *I* am *the Lord: that* is *my name: and my glory will I not give to another, neither my praise to graven images.*
>
> Isaiah 42:8

This is God the Father speaking about His Son. God is not going to share His glory with you. He is not drawing people to you. He is drawing people to His Son.

The moment a leader starts drawing people to themselves, that shows you they are not a godly leader. There are many leaders in the world today, but they are often promoting and magnifying themselves. They are not drawing people to Jesus through their leadership.

When I was a kid, my dad used to say, "He that tooteth not his own horn, the same shall not be tooted." He said that often enough, I grew up thinking it was a scripture! Now, I know that was just a joke, but for a lot of people, that's their "life verse." They think, *If I don't promote myself, nobody else will.*

There was a man in the 1980s who may have had the largest ministry on earth at that time. He was on television and filling arenas, and people were giving him millions of dollars a month. But then he fell into sexual sin and destroyed everything he built.

I remember watching the broadcast where he confessed everything, and what he said really stuck with me. This man said that through television he was reaching more people than Jesus, which is a bold statement all by itself. But then this man said that because of the success and the amount of influence he was having, he thought he could do anything.

That right there was the problem—he wasn't dependent on God anymore. And he ended up losing his influence by trying to satisfy his lusts. If you want God to be the one who exalts you, flows through you, and allows you to lead other people, you're going to have to learn how to humble yourself and put God and others first.

I can think of many examples of people who started out in their ministry or business dependent on God. And yet, when the Lord began to bless and increase them, they forgot all about Him. They forgot about the One who took them that far.

These people became self-sufficient and started leaning on their own understanding (Prov. 3:5). And many of those same people who trusted in God when they were small eventually crashed and burned because they quit being God dependent.

On that night in 1968, I had such a revelation of God, who He is, and my relative unworthiness, that I humbled myself. I made my life and ministry totally dependent on my relationship with Him. You may not need a supernatural experience like I had, but I guarantee that you need to recognize your place in relationship to God in such a way that you never get over it.

Contention Comes by Pride

> *Only by pride cometh contention: but with the well advised* is *wisdom.*
>
> Proverbs 13:10

This verse makes it clear that pride is the source of all contention. I know that a lot of people don't want to hear this, but it's not their circumstances or personalities that cause them grief—it's their pride. In case that's confusing, the Hebrew word translated "*only*" in this verse means "only"![13] So, pride is not a leading cause of contention. It's the only cause!

However, pride is like a stick—it has two ends. Most people can clearly see the end that represents arrogance and haughtiness, but they fail to see the other end—low self-esteem, false humility, timidity, or shyness. It all comes back to being focused on ourselves, our feelings, and our needs.

Numbers 12:3 says,

> *Now the man Moses was very meek, above all the men which* were *upon the face of the earth.*

This is one of the most amazing statements in the Bible. And it's even more amazing when you realize Moses was the person who wrote it!

In the previous verses, Moses' brother and sister Aaron and Miriam spoke against him and said, "*Hath the Lord indeed spoken only by Moses? hath he not spoken also by us?*" Moses could have defended himself. He had heard the voice at the burning bush, seen all these great works of God, and led millions of people out of Egypt. It was clear he was a leader. But that would have been a response out of pride, not humility, and that is not a quality of a *godly* leader.

Instead, he wrote, "*Moses* was *very meek, above all the men which were upon the face of the earth.*" This is probably mentioned in reference to the fact that Moses didn't actually say anything in defense of himself. The Lord heard what Aaron and Miriam said and responded on Moses' behalf, making it clear that he was the man God would speak through (Num. 12:4–8). And once He was done speaking, Miriam turned leprous (Num. 12:9–10).

One of the qualities of meekness is not being self-sufficient or quick to defend yourself. Moses was quick to defend the Lord, but he let God defend him. If we defend ourselves, God doesn't. If we leave the judgment up to the Lord, He will do a better job than we ever could (Rom. 12:19). God ended up striking Miriam with leprosy for coming against Moses, which convinced Aaron to repent and ask God for mercy (Num. 12:11–12).

When Moses said he was the meekest man on the face of the earth, that was an accurate assessment. God inspired him to write it, and it would have been prideful of Moses to disagree. But most people think if you were truly humble, you certainly wouldn't admit it the way Moses did.

False Humility

I can do all things through Christ which strengtheneth me.

Philippians 4:13

Religion has warped our perception of true humility. It's taught that humility is weakness or low self-esteem—an attitude of self-abasement and timidity. Religious humility says, "I am nothing and I can do nothing." According to what the church has portrayed, a truly humble person would never even acknowledge they were humble the way Moses did.

I heard a story about a man who was honored by his church for being its most humble member. The church got together and made him a huge button that said "Humble" and presented it to him one Sunday. But when they gave him the button, he didn't refuse or deflect their praise. So, they turned around and took the button away! They said if he was truly humble, he wouldn't have accepted it.

You see, people in the church will often portray a false humility when they're singled out for their talents. For example, a person who is asked to sing a special song during a service may say, "The Lord says to make a joyful noise, so that's what I'm going to do today. You all pray for me. I know I don't have a great voice, but I'm going to make a joyful noise."

Then, that same person gets up and sings with a trained operatic voice that shakes the rafters! They weren't actually being humble. They were fishing for a compliment! It was done in the hopes that someone would come up to them afterward and say, "You have a wonderful voice!"

Things like that are a religious con. I'm sure that if you saw that same person in the grocery store and said, "I heard you on Sunday and you were terrible," they wouldn't just respond, "Yes, you're right." No, they'd probably be offended! That's because they were only *pretending* to be humble for everyone in church.

Now, if I'm really being humble, I can say, "I can do nothing," as long as I also say, "without God." And that's true. Without God, I'm like a zero with the rim knocked off. But it's also true that, as a Christian, I'm never without God (Heb. 13:5). That's why I can say, "*I can do all things through Christ.*"

Today, by the grace of God, I have gone from being an introvert who couldn't look at a person in the face and talk to them, to reaching a potential audience of more than six billion people worldwide through our *Gospel Truth* television program. And without God, none of that would have been possible.

Chapter 6

Let God Promote You

For whosoever exalteth himself shall be abased; and he that humbleth himself shall be exalted.

Luke 14:11

Jesus told a parable about a man who had a feast (Luke 14:7–11). He said the man invited all of these people and watched as they came in. They began promoting themselves to sit as close to the host as possible. They wanted seats of honor. But the Lord said that's not the way the kingdom of God operates.

In these kinds of situations, a Christian ought to assume a lower seat. That way, the host won't have to humiliate you and embarrass themselves by asking you to move if a dignitary comes in. Instead, in taking the lower place, the host might end up saying, "Come up higher and take a place next to me."

I've seen this happen in my own life. When I first got started in ministry, I remember trying to prove that I was right. I thought I was just sharing the truth with people, but it was really about me needing to feel secure. When someone said something that countered what I taught, I had to win the argument to feel like I was right. If I couldn't feel right, then it shook my faith in what I was believing.

During that time, my friend Joe Nay really blessed me. He gave me a word from the Lord and said he saw me as if I were running a race on a track. I was out in front, leading the pack, but there were people yelling at me from the grandstands and saying I was doing it all wrong. Joe said he saw me getting off the track and going into the stands to argue with the crowd. He told me, "You may win the argument, but you will lose the race."

Sometime later, I was attending a meeting where Joe was ministering. Before each of his sessions, Joe would call me on stage. I wasn't ministering, but he invited me to greet the people and say something.

On the last night of those meetings, I was invited on stage again. And, in front of hundreds of people, a man I knew came running up to me. He apologized and said, "I've been telling people that you're of the devil! For days, you've been coming up here, and this whole time God has been convicting me of the things I've said about you." He was begging for my forgiveness, crying, and even kissing my boots. It was quite a spectacle!

Now, if I had fought back against those kinds of accusations, there's no way I would have gotten that kind of reaction. I humbled myself, God convicted this man, and our relationship was put back together. I let God exalt me. I humbled myself and focused on my relationship with the Lord, allowing Him to call me up to a higher place.

Take Your Time

Back when my meetings were smaller, I used to spend time ministering to people individually. I'd often give them prophecies and pray over them. Now, I don't do that as much because our meetings are much larger, and I don't have time to meet with everyone. We've since trained prayer ministers to handle a lot of the one-on-one ministry that I used to do.

Years ago, I was in a church, ministering to pastors, and I asked people to come up for prayer. There was a line of about twenty people and this one man was first in line. When I stepped off the platform, I just didn't feel like I should pray for him. So, I skipped him and started ministering to the second person. I went down the row and prophesied to every one of the other ministers there.

When I got down to the end of the row, this man had come around the line and was standing there. When I saw him, I just turned around and started walking back up on the platform. That's when he grabbed me and asked, "Why won't you pray for me?" And I said, "You don't want me to pray for you." But he responded, "Yes, I do! I want anything that God has for me!"

So, I began to prophesy to him. I said, "The reason God's not using you is because you are not usable. It would destroy you and ruin your ministry if you got the opportunities you are seeking." I went on to say, "You don't have the maturity. You need to just stay in the presence of God and grow. And when you get to the place where God can use you, He'll open up the doors."

It turns out this man had come out from a homosexual lifestyle. He believed he was led to minister to homosexuals, but he just wasn't ready for it. He wasn't that far along in his relationship with God to be ready for that kind of ministry. It seemed like he received what I was saying, but when the first opportunity came along, he kicked down the door. He tried to make ministry happen in his own strength. And he went ahead of God.

The last time I saw this man, he had totally turned against the Lord. He was so bitter because things didn't work out the way he wanted them to. It was exactly like what I had said to him in that meeting. He just wasn't ready. He didn't humble himself and wait for due time to be exalted by God.

Wait for God's Best

> *Delight thyself also in the Lord; and he shall give thee the desires of thine heart.*
>
> Psalm 37:4

Carrie Pickett is the Executive Vice President of our ministry along with her husband Mike, and they oversee all of our Charis Bible Colleges around the world. She teaches one of the best things I've ever heard on the subject of humility.

She was raised in the little town of Kit Carson, Colorado, and grew up in Lawson Perdue's church. That's where she first learned about our ministry. Later, she attended Charis Bible College and eventually left everything she knew to become a missionary to Russia in her early 20s. She was instrumental in building up the Charis campuses in that country.

I heard her say one time that when most people think about their lives, it's like they write on a sheet of paper everything they are looking for in a mate, ministry, and life—all of their desires. And then, at the bottom of the page, they sign their name, present it to the Lord, and ask Him to sign it.

That's just the way that most people live. They give God a list of everything they want and then try to draw God into a contract. They just want the Lord to bless whatever they're doing without really finding out what He wants for their life.

But Carrie teaches that if the Lord were to meet with us, He would take a blank sheet of paper, push it across the table, and say, "Now you sign this, and let Me fill in the details." And that's exactly what Carrie did! She sought God and waited for His very best for her life.

Because she humbled herself, Carrie was obedient to the Lord when He called her to Russia. And while she was there, she ended up meeting Mike, who was also an American and a Christian. Carrie left her home and everything she knew, trusting that the Lord had the very best in store for her—even though she couldn't see it herself. She trusted that God would give her the desires of her heart; not just what she desired, but God's desires would become her desires.

Everything in our ministry has come about because I humbled myself. I realized God is smarter and wiser than I am. I just let His desires become my desires. And those are the things I pursued. We don't just follow trends and do what other ministries are doing. It's not that what they are doing isn't good, but I'm not going to do something unless I believe the Lord has told me to do it. I let Him place a desire in my heart, and I follow through on it.

The Lord will not just force you to do anything. You have to choose to be obedient to His will. And that begins with humbling yourself.

Principle III

Character and Integrity

Chapter 7

You Have Influence

> When *pride cometh, then cometh shame: but with the lowly is wisdom. The integrity of the upright shall guide them: but the perverseness of transgressors shall destroy them.*
>
> Proverbs 11:2–3

If you're going to be a godly leader, you need to have character and integrity. This is something missing in most people who call themselves leaders. But I believe no one is exempt from this responsibility. A person's relationship with the Lord is what produces that character and integrity in them. It's just a natural result of relationship.

For example, when a person is married, they prioritize their relationship with their spouse, which sets healthy boundaries for their life. Before I got married, I used to be concerned about what girls thought about me, just like any young guy. But once I was married, I didn't care what anybody else thought about me—*only Jamie!*

Similarly, as you become a disciple of God's Word (John 8:31), you will see the boundaries the Lord has set for your life. You'll only care about what God thinks, and not the rest of the world. You'll stay focused on what *He* has called you to do. That's character and integrity.

Every one of us is a leader in some way. I tell this to our Charis Bible College students all the time. Some of them think they are not leaders. But I remind them that they do have influence. And really, that's what makes someone a leader. There is always someone who looks to you as an example.

When they leave our main campus here in Woodland Park, Colorado, they go out into the community wearing their lanyard and badge that shows they're a Bible college student, or they have a Charis sticker on their car. They have jobs, shop for groceries, and buy gas. They interact with people on a daily basis.

Whether they know it or not, our students are influencing people—either for good or bad. I have people compliment me on a lot of our students. They say things like, "Charis students are the hardest workers," "They're the nicest people," or "They're the biggest tippers." And that's good. But then I've had other people come to me and say the opposite!

Whether it's your own family, the people you go to church with, the people you work with, the people you do business with, or your neighbors, you are influencing somebody. And to be a godly leader, you need to have character and integrity.

The serpent's temptation to Eve in the Garden of Eden was, "*In the day ye eat* [of the tree] *thereof, then your eyes shall be opened, and ye shall be as gods, knowing good and evil*" (Gen. 3:5). People may not realize it, but this is what's happening in our society today. Based on their behavior, many people have made themselves their own gods, determining right from wrong for themselves. And their character and integrity reflect that.

Healthy Boundaries

> *The integrity of the upright shall guide them: but the perverseness of transgressors shall destroy them.*
>
> Proverbs 11:3

When you submit yourself to God, that puts boundaries in your life. And God's Word informs you of those boundaries. That's why it's so important for us to renew our minds according to the Word (Rom. 12:2). It determines a person's character and integrity.

For example, the Bible says that homosexuality is a sin (Lev. 18:22). It's an abomination, and yet people today are saying, "We are proud of it." They are bragging about it and holding parades. They've rejected the God of the Bible, and they've established their own standards. Among other things, they're for transgenderism and giving children hormone blockers and sex reassignment surgeries. That's just demonic.

This kind of behavior and belief system is perverse and destructive. People who support these things have made themselves their own gods. That is not having character and integrity. That's living outside the boundaries God has set for our lives.

Because I've submitted myself to God and His Word, homosexuality is out of bounds for me. Transgenderism is out of bounds. Adultery is out of bounds. Lying and stealing are out of bounds. Murder is out of bounds.

My relationship with God automatically sets limits in my life. I don't have to get up every day and decide if I'm going to be following God. I made that decision when I got born again as an eight-year-old and later made a total commitment of my life to the Lord when I supernaturally encountered Him on March 23, 1968. Now, I haven't done everything perfectly. I've missed it from time to time. But my heart has always been to do what's right.

Once, I recorded some television programs that didn't have the desired effect I had hoped for. I didn't set out to disobey God, but I just wasn't bold in what I believed He asked me to do. I repented, went to the Lord, and said, "I've made a mess of things, but I was a mess when You met me, and I know that You love me!" I could say that because my commitment is to God first over anything or anyone else, including myself. And to the best of my ability, that's how I try to live.

I don't think that any Christian just gets up in the morning and thinks, *Today, I'm going to commit adultery. I'm going to lie. I'm going to steal. I'm going to reject my faith in the Lord.* No one who's born again plans on those things happening. But if a person doesn't have character and integrity—if they don't have these boundaries in their life, set by God's Word—they get into situational ethics and compromise because the pressure on them is greater than the emphasis they've put on their own relationship with God.

Obey God

Many Christians may know what God wants them to do but they don't always obey. Instead, their actions are based on what they think the consequences will be. If they think something bad will happen by following God's plan, they won't do it.

During Covid, I had a guy come to me who was a nurse. This man said the hospital he worked at told him he would be fired if he didn't take the vaccine. I asked, "Well, do you think you're supposed to take the vaccine?" He said, "No! God told me not to do it." (Now, I'm not discussing whether or not *you* should take a vaccine; I'm just saying God told *him* not to take that vaccine.) I said, "Well, if God told you not to do it, don't do it." His immediate response was, "But they're going to fire me!" And I said, "What does that matter? If God tells you to do something, you just do it!"

John Quincy Adams, the sixth president of the United States, is popularly believed to have said, "Duty is ours; results are God's."[4] We should never debate doing what the Lord has instructed us to do because of a fear of what might happen or what other people may say. Ultimately, the decision to do or not do something should be based on our relationship with God.

Many people rely on situational ethics. In other words, if they feel the situation justifies compromising what they believe, they will. Similarly, if they think no one will know what they are doing, they are more likely to just give in to their carnal desires.

When I was serving in Vietnam, there was another guy there who grew up with me. We went to church together and knew each other our entire lives. We weren't stationed in the exact same spot, but we saw each other occasionally.

The U.S. military would regularly bring troops out of the field for what they called a "stand down." And for three days, they would give them all the alcohol they could drink. They also brought in women and put on a musical show that was sexually suggestive. It turned out that those women were prostitutes. So, a person could have all of the booze, drugs, and sex they wanted.

This man I grew up with wasn't a fanatic about God, but he was born again. He would've never participated in anything like that back in the States, because it would've been a reflection on his family. But in Vietnam, he did. Even though he had the same upbringing as I did, this guy wound up giving in to temptation.

I believe that's the case with many people who suffer from post-traumatic stress disorder. They are not only dealing with the terrible things they saw in combat but also the things they did when they compromised their morals. They just hadn't developed character and integrity as part of a living relationship with God. They didn't have boundaries.

Chapter 8

Keep Your Promises

The transgression of the wicked saith within my heart, that there is *no fear of God before his eyes.*

Psalm 36:1

People who don't have a relationship with the Lord just don't have any restrictions in their life. They're like water. They just seek the lowest level and follow the path of least resistance. That's not character. That's not integrity.

If you're one of those people who's always got your finger up in the air trying to discern which way the wind of public opinion is blowing, you do not need to be a leader. If you're just going to do whatever is convenient, you shouldn't be a leader.

There are very few godly leaders today, but there are plenty of people in leadership who have been corrupted by this kind of thinking. And many people who started right will eventually compromise. It's because they prioritize the approval of people over their relationship with God.

For example, people who get elected to public office, like state legislature or Congress, seek to be appointed to committees so they can have influence. They do this to claim that they've done something and get reelected. But that often requires allowing themselves to be influenced by party leaders, lobbyists, and other people. As a result, some of them start compromising and doing things contrary to godly principles.

Once, a friend of mine helped get a certain politician elected as a lawmaker. This person promised that they were going to be conservative on the issues and vote a certain way. But when they got into office, they flip-flopped on their positions and started voting for things like abortion. They started doing things against what they had promised during their campaign.

This friend of mine, who put his weight behind that politician and helped get them elected, asked, "Why are you doing these things? You broke your word to us." And that politician said, "You do not understand the pressure once you get here, and all of the things that go on. I don't want to do it, but I've got to do it. There's no option."

Now, I believe there's always an option. But even though this person wanted to do what was right, they compromised their character and integrity based on getting reelected. That's not the way it should be. And people like that fear men more than they fear God. They are looking for honor from men more than they're looking for honor from God (John 5:44). It all goes back to relationship.

I believe that if you asked people whether their elected officials need to have character and integrity, the majority would agree. They want people who will stand on their principles and keep their promises. But if they don't honor God more than they honor people, they'll just wind up doing whatever it takes to get ahead.

The Precious Life

> *For by means of a whorish woman* a man is brought *to a piece of bread: and the adulteress will hunt for the precious life.*
>
> Proverbs 6:26

You may wonder what this scripture has to do with leadership. Well, Satan uses a lot of the same tactics, whether it's in a home, business, government, or ministry. He's after "*the precious life*," and as Jesus said, "*the thief* [Satan] *cometh not, but for to steal, and to kill, and to destroy*" (John 10:10).

When I was in the Army, I had trouble saluting people. In the States, I was repeatedly reprimanded for it, but I finally got the message. I remember when I first got to Vietnam as a private first class, I was stationed on a fire support base. I saw a lieutenant coming across the hill. I saluted him as we passed by each other.

Without warning, the officer threw me on the ground, put his foot on my throat, and said, "Trooper, if you ever see this bald head coming, you better run the other way. Because if you salute me again, I'll kill you!" And all I could think was, *Which is it?* I didn't understand if I was supposed to salute or not. I was totally confused.

As it turned out, there were snipers surrounding the fire support base and it was a dangerous situation. I learned that when soldiers are out in the field, snipers will look for the person who's in charge—an officer. They don't shoot the enlisted men. They go for the person who's the leader. When I was saluting this lieutenant, I was tipping off the snipers about who was "*the precious life*" on that base.

The enemy goes for people who are leaders. When God promotes someone, they have greater influence, making them a larger target for the devil's attacks. This is one reason why God doesn't immediately promote some people. It's because He loves us and doesn't want to raise anyone above the level of their character.

If you haven't been promoted where you are at, it may be that you haven't yet developed your relationship with God. You aren't truly submitted to Him. And if you get under pressure, you're liable to do whatever you think you need to do to deal with that pressure. If you lack character and integrity, it will cause you to depart from what God made you to be.

God loves you so much that He doesn't want to put you in a position that is going to make you crack under pressure. So, until you develop your relationship with the Lord and humble yourself to where He's God and you aren't, you might not yet have the character and integrity to withstand the pressure that comes with promotion.

Make Yourself Usable

> *And* [Jesus] *said, Whereunto shall we liken the kingdom of God? or with what comparison shall we compare it?* It is *like a grain of mustard seed, which, when it is sown in the earth, is less than all the seeds that be in the earth: but when it is sown, it groweth up, and becometh greater than all herbs, and shooteth out great branches; so that the fowls of the air may lodge under the shadow of it.*
>
> Mark 4:30–32

Within a short period of time after my encounter with the Lord on March 23, 1968, I knew that what God had revealed to me was for more people than just me. I wanted to share it with everybody I possibly could. So, I started heading in that direction.

One day, as I was reading these verses, I said, "God, I want you to touch my life and use me so I can touch people all over the world." I had no idea I'd be reaching millions of people around the world through television and Charis Bible College, but I had the desire for it. So, I was just praying, "God, I want to be this huge tree that reaches out to touch and bless people."

That's when the Lord spoke to me and said, "If I were to answer your prayer today and give you this worldwide ministry that you desire, the first bird that landed on one of your branches would cause the whole thing to fall over because your root is about an inch deep." I wouldn't have been able to withstand the pressures and persecution that come with serving the Lord.

God told me not to worry about the growth people see above ground but to focus on getting myself rooted in the Word of God. He also told me, "Quit praying 'God use me,' and instead pray, 'God make me usable.'" So, that's what I did. I just planted the seed of God's Word (1 Pet. 1:23) in my heart and determined to let the Lord make me usable.

For the next thirty years, I pastored three small churches, taught a circuit of six Bible studies in three states, was in traveling ministry, went on radio, and just did everything I could to serve God. But it was all a progression. As I matured in the Lord, He gave me more responsibility to minister His Word.

Then, the Lord woke me up at 3:05 a.m. on July 26, 1999, and said, "The time has come." And all I could say was, "The time has come *for what*?" That's when God told me I was just then beginning my ministry as we planned to go on television the following year. That was discouraging and encouraging at the same time. I had already been pursuing God's will for thirty years, but I knew He never served dessert first—so great things were on their way.

Chapter 9

Prepare Yourself

The preparations of the heart in man, and the answer of the tongue, is *from the Lord.*

Proverbs 16:1

I remember one student at our Bible college who was really enthusiastic about evangelism. He would witness to anybody and everybody. He could get a fencepost born again! As a matter of fact, his classmates chose him to be the class speaker because he was so dynamic.

Once, I was teaching in one of my classes about taking time to prepare yourself and build your character and integrity, and this man stood up and rebuked me! He told me the number of people who die every single day without knowing about the Lord and that they go into a Christless eternity. He said, "I haven't got three years, five years, or ten years to wait. I've got to go do it now!"

This man said he had a revelation from God that he would lead one million people to Christ with the Gospel. That's a great desire. Satan didn't put that in his heart. I believe this man got a glimpse of what the Lord wanted for his life, but he was unwilling to wait.

He was making the point that the need to evangelize outweighed the need to prepare himself for ministry. Now, part of what he was saying is true—people do need to hear the Gospel. But he also needed time to prepare himself so he could share that message for years to come. I told this man, "Preparation time is never wasted time. You need to just be patient. Instead of kicking the door down, you need to let God open a door that no man can shut" (Rev. 3:8).

This is one of the reasons we tell people that they need to come to Charis Bible College. Instead of having to learn everything through the "school of hard knocks," there is a better way. You can learn through the collected experience of all our instructors.

If you try to make things come to pass rather than take the time to prepare yourself, you probably aren't going to fulfill what God has called you to do. Godly leaders should spend time preparing themselves for what's to come.

Sad to say, this man ended up quitting school because he was so adamant about needing to do something right away. And that's been more than twenty years ago. I don't know if he's making any impact for the kingdom of God, but if he would have brought a million people to Christ by now, I likely would have heard about it! He certainly would have been better off being patient and letting God work in his life to prepare him.

Don't Take Shortcuts

There were times I could have done certain things to circumvent the growth process God was leading me through. But it would have required me to compromise my character and integrity, which is something I would not do.

For years we struggled financially. Our income seemed to fluctuate every month. We had creditors calling us, and it got so bad that my staff was afraid to answer the phone. At one point, my board even told me I should shut down the ministry.

So, when I was contacted by some people who said they could raise funds for our ministry, I was ready to listen. These people told me they wrote a fundraising letter for another well-known minister, sent it to his mailing list, and saw it generate $22 million.

My ministry was a lot smaller back then, so they couldn't guarantee me those kinds of results. But they said, "We will guarantee you $1 million if you'll buy our services and let us send out an appeal letter." I sure could have used that kind of money, so I read what they prepared for me.

Their letter said our ministry had orphanages. It showed pictures of babies with swollen bellies and flies on their faces. It also claimed we had all kinds of other projects, but I said, "Those things aren't true!"

They responded by saying, "It wasn't true about this other ministry we wrote for, but it still got them money. It doesn't matter how you get the money; you just take it and then use it however you want to. But this will get you money!" So, I kicked those people out of my office.

I also once visited a large media ministry, and a guy took me into a huge room where they had letters stacked up to the ceiling. I asked, "What are these?" And he said, "These are our crisis letters for three years in advance." There were no crises yet, but they had written about them to manipulate people into giving.

They justified those letters by saying, "If we don't send out these letters and tell people there's a crisis, then we're actually going to have one." They just made up these crises and that's how they raised money.

Because of things like these, people have gotten to where they don't trust a lot of media ministers. But I have a relationship with God, and because of that, I have boundaries set in my life. I wasn't going to lie to people and manipulate them to get money. I had already decided that God was my source, and I believed Him for the finances we needed.

When I was tempted with shortcuts to get finances, I had the character and integrity to resist them. Those things were out of bounds. And it wasn't long after these things that I started getting a revelation on prosperity that allowed our ministry to grow and do the things God wanted to do through us.

Be Faithful with Little

> *His lord said unto him, Well done, good and faithful servant; thou hast been faithful over a few things, I will make thee ruler over many things: enter thou into the joy of thy lord.*
>
> Matthew 25:23

Back when the Lord spoke to me on July 26, 1999, He said that if I had died or quit before going on television, I would have missed His will for my life. That's what God meant when He said, "The time has come." It's not that I had been out of the will of God; I had just been in preparation for all those years. I was entering into His perfect will (Rom. 12:2).

I remember years before, back in the 1980s and 90s, I just went full force into trying to develop a media ministry. At the time, I was on the radio, broadcasting on up to 150 stations. That was awesome, but I knew there was more.

I just couldn't understand why things weren't happening as quickly as I wanted them to. But it takes time to see God's will come to pass. The Lord couldn't just take me from where I was to where I was supposed to be in just one step.

Again, we had been struggling financially, which put a limit on what we could do. So, in the mid-1990s, I wrote down one hundred scriptures about financial prosperity on a yellow legal pad and meditated on them for two years. Then, in 1996, a man came to speak at Charis Bible College who was really strong in that area. It turned out that everything he was teaching was what I had already been meditating on for those two years, and those scriptures came alive on the inside of me.

The results were almost immediate. We went from just breaking even on every meeting we hosted to bringing in two and a half times the budget in the following meeting. Things changed dramatically! But because I had spent time preparing my heart and leaning on my relationship with God, I was ready to handle that responsibility.

Soon, the Lord began talking to me about going on television. We started with a $70,000 budget and a single camera, which seemed ambitious for us back then. Now, we're spending millions of dollars every month on our *Gospel Truth* daily program and Gospel Truth Network.

These days, I can just cast all the care of that over on the Lord (1 Pet. 5:7). But if I had tried to handle that same responsibility years ago, it would have destroyed me. I hadn't fully developed my character and integrity to where it needed to be. I had to grow in my relationship with the Lord and handle the little things before I could be trusted with much.

Principle IV

Hear God's Voice

Chapter 10

The Good Shepherd

To him the porter openeth; and the sheep hear his voice: and he calleth his own sheep by name, and leadeth them out. And when he putteth forth his own sheep, he goeth before them, and the sheep follow him: for they know his voice. And a stranger will they not follow, but will flee from him: for they know not the voice of strangers.

John 10:3–5

Many people really think that they are God's gift to the world. When God shows them that He wants to use them, they think, *Okay, God, I can handle it from here. You just get me introduced, put me on the stage, and I'll do the rest.*

People who have natural talents and abilities tend to depend upon their own selves and don't hear the voice of God. But if you can't hear God's voice, what business do you have leading anyone? Nobody needs to be following your carnal self.

If you are in relationship with God, He will speak to you. This is an absolutely essential quality for being a godly leader. You need to be able to hear and be led by God's voice and not just do your own thing.

In these verses, Jesus was speaking about Himself as the Good Shepherd. In the same chapter, He said, "*My sheep hear my voice*" (John 10:27) and will not follow the voice of a stranger. This is the opposite of most people's experience.

Most people can hear the devil all of the time. They'll listen to the slightest whisper of doubt, unbelief, or fear. But they say they have trouble hearing God's voice. And yet, Jesus said His sheep hear His voice. Something's wrong with this picture!

This all comes back to a person's relationship with the Lord. The reason believers aren't hearing the voice of God is because they aren't in fellowship with Him. They aren't in close communion with Him.

The truth is most people spend more time in the light of their televisions than they do in the light of God's Word. They pay hundreds of dollars every month to have the sewage of the world pumped into their homes and personal devices. People are just being inundated with filth, lies, and propaganda.

For example, I've heard that Americans spend an average of four and a half hours every day looking at things on their cell phones.[5] It's no wonder why people say they can't hear the voice of God. He can't get a word in edgewise!

Cut the Background Noise

> *And in the morning, rising up a great while before day,* [Jesus] *went out, and departed into a solitary place, and there prayed.*
>
> Mark 1:35

Years ago, I was in Washington, DC, not long after President Ronald Reagan died. They brought his body to the Capitol building so it could lie in state. We just happened to be there during that time, so we went through the Rotunda and took part in that.

Later, as we were walking on the gravel paths around the National Mall, I couldn't hear a single step that I was making. I just happened to notice, and thought, *This is strange. I know this is bound to be making noise, but I can't hear myself walking on this gravel.* It's not something I would typically think about, so I believe it was God who brought it to my attention.

After we got done in Washington, we went to the Shenandoah National Park, which is more than an hour's drive outside the city. While I was there, walking on the Appalachian Trail, I could hear every leaf and twig I stepped on. It was so loud that it seemed it was echoing.

The Appalachian Trail was so quiet that I could clearly hear every step I took. That's because no one else was around. In contrast, my footsteps on the Mall were drowned out by all the traffic and activity around us. I realized that it was because there were planes, buses, cars, and tour groups in the city. There was so much ambient noise that I couldn't hear my footsteps. They were drowned out by all of those other sounds.

In the forest, with no one else around, little things like leaves and twigs sounded loud by comparison. The Lord spoke to me through that experience. He showed me that this is why people don't hear Him. They get caught up in the busyness of the world, and it drowns out the voice of God.

Again, to be a godly leader you've got to hear His voice. And it comes by getting quiet and spending time with God alone, away from all the noise and distractions of this world. Jesus liked to be alone with His Father, and so do I.

This is one of the reasons why, for years, I would go for walks nearly every day near my home. We live in the mountains of Colorado, and when I got out on those trails in the woods, that allowed me to pray, praise, and just commune with God. Some of the most important revelations I've received and decisions I've made concerning this ministry came about during those walks.

Be Still and Know

> *Be still, and know that I* am *God: I will be exalted among the heathen, I will be exalted in the earth.*
>
> Psalm 46:10

One of the ways God speaks to people is through dreams. Some people don't put any importance on dreams at all, but God speaks to me through dreams all of the time. It would be unusual to go a week without God revealing something to me in dreams.

I'm what they call a lucid dreamer. When I dream, I sometimes can't tell whether I'm asleep or whether I'm awake. That's because my brain is working while I'm asleep just as much as it is when I'm awake.

Years ago, I had a dream where I saw this huge banner that read, "Psalm 46:10." Even though I had quoted that verse probably hundreds of times, in this dream I could not think of what it said. So, I woke up, got my Bible, and looked it up. As a result, I figured that God was speaking something to me about being still.

At the time, we were living in a place that was so remote and secluded that I couldn't even see another house. That day, Jamie went into town to do some shopping. So, I decided to use that time alone to find out what the Lord was trying to show me. I wasn't sure exactly what it meant to "*be still, and know that I am God.*" But just to be sure, I was determined to be physically still, not just mentally and emotionally still.

I went outside and sat on the deck in a chair. Then I put my hands on my legs, and I didn't move for about an hour and a half. All I did was blink. I was so still that a deer came up to me. It nearly put its nose up to my nose! Deer have poor eyesight, so if you are downwind and they can't pick up your scent, they may get close to you. But this was unusual!

I had chipmunks crawl up my legs because I was so still. I saw thousands of ants. I could hear the wind blowing through the trees and making noise. I could even hear crows flapping their wings as they flew by. These things were happening all around me, but I usually didn't notice them.

The Lord showed me that it's in being still that we really get to know Him. That doesn't necessarily mean just sitting still and not moving. But it is talking about removing all of the noise and distractions from your life that just drown out the voice of God.

Chapter 11

Trust in the Lord

Trust in the L*ORD* *with all thine heart; and lean not unto thine own understanding. In all thy ways acknowledge him, and he shall direct thy paths.*

Proverbs 3:5–6

There are a lot of people who think they are smarter than God. They know God told them to do one thing, but they think it'd be much better if they did something else instead. They lean on their own understanding. But these verses are talking about drawing on your relationship with God.

When you have a living relationship with God, you won't lean on your own understanding. You'll be willing to believe He is smarter and wiser than you are. You'll follow His directions. You will place limitations and restrictions on who you give your attention to. And as you do that, you'll be more likely to listen to God's voice only. You won't just follow any voice.

The Hebrew word translated as "*acknowledge him*" (Prov 3:6), is the word *yâda'*, which means "to know" God in an intimate sense.[6] So, acknowledging God isn't just recognizing that He exists. This is talking about intimacy, like in a relationship. That means if you have a poor relationship with God, you're going to have a poor record of hearing Him speak to you.

God isn't wanting you to lead in your own strength and wisdom. God wants to touch your life. The Lord wants to have a relationship with you more than He wants to use you. God loves you more than what you can do for Him. But there are still a lot of people who admit that they don't spend much time with the Lord.

Many people have their lives full of other things they consider more important than God. They just don't make time for Him. Their relationship with the Lord is struggling and yet they're trying to get a word from Him. They are trying to understand what He wants them to do without investing in their relationship with Him.

That's not the way that it works. You don't have the Lord just speak to you and use you out of the blue. You have to grow in your relationship with Him. And hearing God's voice comes out of that relationship.

There are times that Jamie speaks into my life in a way that no one else can. That's because we have a relationship with each other that we just don't have with everyone else. I believe the Lord specifically put us together. And there is no one else in this world who would have gone through the things that Jamie has and stuck with me. She's been a blessing.

It is really important that you hear God's voice and not somebody else's voice. There are many voices in this world today. And not every thought or desire that you have is from God.

Listen in the Spirit

> *God* is *a Spirit: and they that worship him must worship* him *in spirit and in truth.*
>
> John 4:24

Communication with God is Spirit to spirit and not mouth to ear, the way we communicate in the physical realm. The Holy Spirit speaks to our spirits, not in words, but in thoughts and impressions.

The Lord doesn't typically say "You do this or that," but He will impress your spirit to do something. Then, as you draw things out of your spirit, you'll think, *I should do that!* That's actually why many people miss the leading of the Holy Spirit. They think those things are a product of their own thoughts.

In the same way, every one of us has done something stupid and afterward said, "I knew that was the wrong thing to do. I shouldn't have done that." Maybe you didn't feel right about your decision, but you did it anyway only to find that the impression you had was from the Lord. I learned this the hard way while pastoring a little church in Pritchett, Colorado, in the late 1970s.

All the elders of the church were custom combiners. Six months of the year, they were gone during the wheat harvest. They insisted that we ordain another elder who would stay behind to help me as pastor. The man they chose was someone I had nothing against, but something didn't feel right about ordaining him as an elder. However, I dismissed those things and went with logic instead of my heart.

Within two weeks of the others leaving for the wheat harvest, this new elder accused me of stealing money from the church, committing adultery, drinking, smoking, and everything else you can imagine. It was a terrible experience. As soon as this man showed his true colors, I knew that the impression I had was the Spirit speaking to me. I decided that I would never ignore my heart again. I would trust what the Spirit was showing me.

Years later, I was invited to minister in Costa Rica. It was a place I had been to before, and I was excited to go back. Yet, as I prayed about it, I lost my desire to go. To get a better understanding of what the Lord was showing me, I spent seventeen hours on a road trip praying in tongues (1 Cor. 2:7). The more I got my mind focused on the Lord, the less I wanted to go back to Costa Rica. So, I canceled the trip.

When the people who invited me asked why, all I could tell them was I just didn't want to go. That may have caused some hard feelings. But as it turned out, the plane I had booked for my flight crashed on take-off, killing all those on board. The Lord warned me and saved my life, not by saying, "Don't go to Costa Rica," but by communicating to my spirit and changing my desire (Ps. 37:4).

Bring to Remembrance

> *But the Comforter,* which is *the Holy Ghost, whom the Father will send in my name, he shall teach you all things, and bring all things to your remembrance, whatsoever I have said unto you.*
>
> John 14:26

In the early 2000s, Charis Bible College was in a period of significant growth. So much so, that it was outgrowing the 14,600-square-foot facility on Robinson Street in Colorado Springs that housed our ministry, television studio, and school.

In time, we actually ended up finding a building on Elkton Drive that was 110,000 square feet, but only part of it could be used for office space. We had to build out the rest of it for our ministry and Bible college. It was estimated that renovations would cost $3.2 million, and that was on top of the purchase price of $3.25 million, which was a big step for us at the time.

After we purchased the building, we tried to obtain a construction loan for the renovations. And for nine months, we waited. Every time we asked our banker about the loan, he kept telling us we would get it "next week." It was a difficult situation.

Finally, the banker said, "We'll just get a new appraisal and start the whole process over." But all I could see was another nine months of delays. Something didn't seem right. So, I committed to get away with the Lord and pray.

We lived on property with miles of trails, so I decided to take a walk, pray in tongues, and seek an interpretation (1 Cor. 14:13). I've found over the years that God will show me things in the spirit through praying in tongues and interpretation.

I wasn't a hundred yards down that trail before the Lord brought to remembrance some things He had spoken to me two years earlier. Someone had given me a prophecy that I wouldn't need to take out a loan because I already had my own bank.

When the Holy Spirit brought that to my remembrance (John 14:26), I thought, *I have my own bank? Where is it?* Then I recalled the rest of the prophecy—my ministry partners would be my bank! Somehow, I hadn't associated the prophecy with the building program. The Lord said, "I don't want you to take out a loan. I'm going to pay for this."

In just fourteen months, our partners gave the funds we needed, and our ministry and Bible college were using that building. A few years later, we filled that space, and the Lord led us to where we are in Woodland Park. We were able to walk through all those things because we heard His voice and trusted Him.

Chapter 12

Are You There?

And there was a certain disciple at Damascus, named Ananias; and to him said the Lord in a vision, Ananias. And he said, Behold, I am here, *Lord.*

Acts 9:10

Years ago, the Lord spoke to me from this verse. He said, "Andrew, how many times have I called your name, and you weren't there?" Ananias was "there."

If you're His sheep, the Lord speaks to you (John 10:27). God speaks to every one of us every single day. There is never any problem you face that God isn't right there speaking to you. But the question is, are you "there" listening, or are you worrying or in strife? Are you distracted, just being entertained, or are you tuned in to what God is saying to you?

You have to spend time in the presence of the Lord. If you do that, God will speak to you. I don't take very much time off. But when I do, I typically come back with a list of things the Lord showed me concerning our ministry, because I spent time with Him.

This happened a few years ago while driving from Florida to Colorado. We ended up taking eleven days to make the trip. When I got back to our ministry, I had a list of so many things to accomplish that our CEO Billy Epperhart jokingly said, "Don't let him take any more time off!"

Years ago, Jamie and I had the chance to spend time with Oral Roberts in his home just a few months before he died, and it made a huge impact on me. If you know anything about Oral, he placed a strong emphasis on hearing God's voice.

We were only with Oral for a few hours, but I learned a lot from him in that short period of time. It's like when you are traveling. If someone has already driven the same road you're on, it's wise to call that person and ask them some questions. You'd want to know if there are any roadblocks or if there are good places to stop and eat.

There were about twenty ministers there, and one of the questions they asked Oral was, "How do we change a nation?" My ears pricked up because I wanted to hear what this man of God had to say. And when he responded, I thought he shared some great wisdom.

Oral Roberts said, "You can't change a nation, because nobody can change a nation. All we can do is what God tells each of us to do. And if each person does what God tells them to do, He can knit those things together. Because God is the only One who can change a nation."

Why should it be any different in a church, business, or other organization? It will take a godly leader to cast the Lord's vision, but each person has to be "there" hearing from God, trusting Him, and doing their part to be successful.

Stand with God

In the 1970s, when we were really struggling financially, Jamie and I went to a meeting where a man taught about prosperity. What this man was sharing would have radically changed our lives if we had the time to really dig in deep, listen to what he was saying, and meditate on the scriptures he taught.

When we went to the back of the room, we saw resources for sale on biblical prosperity. The only problem was, we didn't have the money to purchase them. It's not that we didn't have *enough* money; we didn't have *any* money! I looked over at Jamie, who was pregnant at the time, and I saw tears well up in her eyes.

I told the Lord in that moment that if He revealed anything to me that would help another person, I would not deny them access to it because of finances. That's when God started speaking to me about giving away our ministry materials at no charge. At the time, there was no model for that. I had never heard of any minister giving everything away. This was the voice of the Lord that came to me. And looking back, I think it's one of the best things I have ever done.

Over the years, we've seen people abuse these things—they would sweep dozens of copies of the same teaching into a shopping bag—and I've even had well-known ministers prophesy to me and say, "Thus saith the Lord, you need to quit giving your things away. You need to start charging for your products!"

I'll admit, we had to set a limit on how many free materials a person could receive in a week, and we tell people they can give a suggested donation for a resource, but we still give away many things at no charge. I've stayed true to what the Lord spoke to me all those years ago.

We quit counting at about 200 million free books, CDs, DVDs, cassette tapes, and other things. And that doesn't include the millions of downloads from our website each month. We've just given all these things away. And all that came from trusting God and standing on what He spoke to me about giving things away.

If the Lord had told me back then that we would give away hundreds of millions of materials, it probably would've overwhelmed me. I'm not sure I would've had enough faith to do all of that, but I was just in relationship with God. It's just something the Lord put on my heart, and I promised to do it even to my own hurt (Ps. 15:4). I just had to trust Him and do my part.

We've found that 50 percent of the people who get materials from our ministry do so because it's free. And, in the healing and financial testimonies we share on our website, people often say they first came in contact with those life-changing truths through our free resources.

Do One Thing Well

> *Brethren, I count not myself to have apprehended: but* this *one thing* I do, *forgetting those things which are behind, and reaching forth unto those things which are before.*
>
> Philippians 3:13

I have people come to me all the time, wanting me to help with their project or some other cause. They may be good things, but they're not things that God called me to do. I've learned to just listen to the Lord and focus on what He's called me to do if I want to be successful

All the enemy has to do to destroy a man's vision is give him two. When you have two visions, that's "di-vision." That's why I walk with the Lord and listen to His voice. I need to clearly hear from God.

Just because something looks good, and I have the resources, doesn't mean I'm supposed to do it. If Satan can't keep you from serving God, then he'll try to get you so busy doing multiple things that you will wear out and be ineffective.

Paul made it clear that he knew what his call was, and he stayed focused on that one thing. These days, people brag about being multitaskers. All that means is they do multiple things less efficiently than they would if they just did one thing.

In our ministry, we have a lot of things going on. Everybody has a lane they are supposed to stay in. Everybody has an assignment. Each has to hear what the Lord is saying about what He has called each of them to do at the ministry.

Years ago, when the ministry was smaller, people seemed to bring me every single issue, so I had to deal with it. I've since learned what my position is as a leader and that I just can't get down in the weeds and deal with those things. I may not see the wisdom of doing something in a certain way, but I also can't micromanage how people do things. I have to hear God's voice and do the things He's called me to do.

Right now, I deal with just five people in a ministry that has about 1,200 employees. And I have to maintain a high-level view of things, so I don't get distracted from what God calls me to do. When I receive something from the Lord, I share it with my executives and ask them, "How are we going to get this done?" Then, they go to their teams with questions, the answers and solutions come back, and we're able to do those things.

If you don't have the kind of relationship with God where you're constantly in communion with Him and He's speaking to you, I guarantee that Satan will get you off track. The enemy will tempt you with good things that aren't God's things.

Principle V

Vision

Chapter 13

Get God's Plan

And the Lord answered me, and said, Write the vision, and make it *plain upon tables, that he may run that readeth it.*

Habakkuk 2:2

Most people want to start leadership with vision. But if your relationship with God is deficient, if you aren't truly humble, if you don't have character and integrity, and if you aren't listening to God's voice, vision won't matter.

Even if God showed you His vision for your life, you'd ruin the whole thing if you went out and tried to do it your way. There are so many examples of this. Not only can we read about these things in the Word of God, but I could give example after example of people I knew personally who went ahead of God.

These were people who had a word from the Lord, but they didn't put their relationship with God first. They took a word and made a paragraph out of it. They decided that they were going to implement God's plans the way that they wanted to.

I remember one guy who came out of a business background, so he had a lot of secular training on how to successfully run things. After he got born again, this man got a revelation on spirit, soul, and body (1

Thess. 5:23), which is one of the things that God used to totally change my life. We actually met because he heard me teaching on it and said he had that same revelation.

This man got a truth from God, but he decided he was going to present it the same way that he had done things back in the business world. So, within days of getting a revelation about his identity in Christ, he took out a loan of tens of thousands of dollars. (This was back in the 1980s, so what he borrowed may be the equivalent of more than $100,000 today!)

He put out this teaching on spirit, soul, and body in a three-ring binder with full-color printing. It looked very professional and was well done. But he spent tens of thousands of dollars on it, put himself in debt, and just thought it was automatically going to work.

This man had a revelation from God that would change lives, and he saw how important it was, but he decided he was going to market it with his worldly business sense. And it just about destroyed him. He couldn't make the debt payments, and his ministry ended up collapsing. Things just never worked out. This is an example of someone who heard something from God and had a vision, but he didn't seek God's plan to get it done.

Pursue the Lord

Vision should be a byproduct of your relationship with God, not something that you think of, and then ask God to put His blessing on.

I have been seeking God with everything I've got since I really got turned on to Him in 1968. And I knew God was going to use me in ministry. As I continued to seek the Lord, I knew that it was going to be a worldwide ministry. I just didn't know how any of it was going to come to pass. I only had a glimpse of the end result.

Now, I never actually pursued having a large ministry. I just focused on my relationship with the Lord, and everything flowed from that. For example, I never pursued being on television. I had people offer me television airtime and I knew that eventually it was going to come, but I also knew that it was going to be expensive. I knew it was going to take another level of effort. It was also going to take time.

Because of those things, I honestly wasn't excited about going on television until the late 1990s when the Lord started speaking to me about it. And once the vision came, that was my focus. But I didn't start out pursuing a vision. I started by pursuing a relationship with God.

In the same way, when it came to starting Charis, I didn't want a Bible college. A lot of people asked me to start one, but I never wanted to, largely because I had met too many Bible school graduates who really annoyed me. They were puffed up with knowledge. But that didn't mean they had a better relationship with God or that they loved Him more than other Christians they looked down on.

I didn't want to be associated with something like that, so I had no desire to start a Bible school even though I have always had a strong desire to disciple people. But in the summer of 1993, I was in Britain and heard a man say that if you aren't training up people to do what God has shown you, you're a failure.

Our time on earth is limited. So, unless a person can take what is in them and reproduce it in others (2 Tim. 2:2), ultimately, they have failed. That's part of the reason why Christians are supposed to make disciples and not just converts (Matt. 28:18–20).

I knew those things were true, so it stirred something in me when I heard someone else preach about it. I thought, *God, how can I equip believers to help them start walking in the abundant life You have made available?* The Lord answered, "A Bible school."

In just a moment, I got excited about having a Bible college. I caught the vision for it. But that didn't happen without first having a relationship with God. Because of that, the Lord spoke to me, and I pursued that vision.

Follow Peace, Not Others

> *And let the peace of God rule in your hearts, to the which also ye are called in one body; and be ye thankful.*
>
> Colossians 3:15

You need your own vision. You're unique. Instead of just copying somebody else's vision, you need to lean on your relationship with the Lord. God will show you what He made you to do.

There is supernatural peace, satisfaction, and anointing that is available in doing what God called you to do. There are a lot of people who are frustrated because they are doing whatever their parents or circumstances have led them to do. They were poured into a mold (Rom. 12:2), and they are just going in a direction that may have nothing to do with what God called them to do.

Growing up, every single person in my family—father, mother, aunts, uncles, and everyone else—was a teacher. That's just what they did. I even had an uncle who was a professor at the University of California at Berkeley. Now, I did have another uncle who was a farmer, but he was the exception.

Being a teacher was the expectation. It was the mold I thought I was going to be poured into. But God never wanted me to be a schoolteacher. It's an honorable profession, but I was called to the ministry and to teach the Word of God (Eph. 4:11–13). That was God's vision for my life.

If I had just continued to go in the direction of being a schoolteacher, because I loved God, I believe He would've blessed it to a degree. But I wouldn't have what I'm experiencing now. We wouldn't have produced thousands of Bible college graduates or reached potentially billions of people through television. You probably would've never heard from me!

Not long after I got a revelation of God's glory and His love for me in 1968, I felt like He told me to leave college. There were a lot of reasons why this didn't seem to make sense, but it ended up being one of the best decisions I ever made.

All the same, I had to overcome the pressure from family and church leaders who didn't believe my vision was from the Lord. But based on Colossians 3:15, I let the peace of God rule in my heart like an umpire, and I made the call to leave school rather than go against what I believed He had called me to do. I had to value my relationship with God more than my relationships with others.

Ultimately, because God gave me a vision, I could better determine which things aligned with fulfilling God's plans. Because of that, I was able to reject things that didn't fit within that vision.

Chapter 14

Go Against the Flow

Woe unto you, when all men shall speak well of you! for so did their fathers to the false prophets.

Luke 6:26

You've got to find out what God specifically called you to do. I believe there are a lot of people who are miserable—who talk about things like "Blue Monday"—because they have to go to work and do something that they really aren't that excited about.

Now, there's nothing wrong with work. The Bible says if you don't work, you don't eat (2 Thess. 3:10). But a lot of people are doing what they are doing just because of money, to have material things, or for the approval of others. And they don't feel like they're doing what God called them to do.

You see, this life is not just a dress rehearsal. This is the real deal. And every single day, you're burning daylight. You are either using time to do something significant and accomplish what God called you to do, or you're just wasting time.

When I minister on these things at my meetings, I'll give an invitation to the audience. I'll say, "If you don't know for sure that you are doing what God created you to do, I want you to stand up and I will pray for you." From my observations, it's not unusual for 80–90 percent of a crowd full of Christians—people who love God, are born again, and are baptized in the Holy Spirit—to stand up. By doing that, they are confessing that they don't know for sure what God has called them to do.

That's because most people seem to live like water, just going with the flow and seeking the path of least resistance. But anybody can float downstream. It takes purpose and vision to turn around, swim upstream, and go against the flow.

There is resistance when you start following God's things. Satan is going to supernaturally fight against you. Jesus said, once the seed of God's Word has been sown, Satan comes immediately to steal it away (Mark 4:15). So, when you receive a vision from the Lord, you are going to have demonic opposition.

If there is no resistance to what you are doing and it seems like everybody is just saying positive things about you, I seriously doubt that you've found God's will for your life. That's because fulfilling the vision He's set for your life is going to require effort.

People are going to criticize you, Satan is going to attack you, and you will be going against the flow. That's just the reality. I often say that if you never run into the devil, it's because you're both headed in the same direction!

Focus on Jesus

> *Looking unto Jesus the author and finisher of* our *faith; who for the joy that was set before him endured the cross, despising the shame, and is set down at the right hand of the throne of God.*
>
> Hebrews 12:2

At the time of this writing, we're in the process of expanding our Charis Bible College campus to include student housing, a student activities center, and more. Because it is taking a lot of effort, it would be easy for me to get so focused on the vision that I neglect my personal relationship with the Lord. But I can truthfully say that even though there's still a lot of work to do, and it may cost as much as $1 billion, I have not been preoccupied with it.

Often, when I take time off, I may spend the entire day just praying, studying the Word, and seeking the Lord. I don't spend that time thinking about all of the things we have to do to build out the Bible college or how to pay for it all. I just get focused on the Lord.

I'll tell you, when you do things this way, it takes all of the pressure off of you. There are some people who have a vision, but they take on all of the burden of it. It's like the weight is on their shoulders to produce results.

Right now, we need over $10 million a month to pay our bills, build out our Charis campus, and broadcast our network on television. But I don't worry about it at all. It's not a pressure on me. I can live that way just as a byproduct of my relationship with the Lord. If it's God's will, then it's His bill!

I am not starting something and trying to get God to bless it. This is the Lord's vision, and He's just asked me to steward it. Because of that, it changes everything. I'm not trying to accomplish these things out of my own strength. I can trust that God will give me strength and provide for everything I need to get the job done through Jesus Christ (Phil. 4:13 and 19).

It all goes back to your personal relationship with the Lord. Everything revolves around that. It's like a wheel: the hub is the center, all of the spokes go out from it, and the rim is on the outside. But it's all dependent upon that hub. If you just have a rim and the spokes, but don't have a hub that they can tie into, the whole thing will fall apart.

Unfortunately, most people will prioritize a vision over everything else. They will start with that spoke and neglect the hub of relationship with God. The vision will fall apart if it's not anchored in their relationship with God. But if they keep their eyes fixed on Jesus, that vision will come to pass.

Stay on Track

> *Where* there is *no vision, the people perish: but he that keepeth the law, happy* is *he.*
>
> Proverbs 29:18

If there is no vision, you won't know where you're going. And if you don't know where you're going, any old road will take you there.

The *New International Version* translation of this same verse says, "*Where there is no revelation, people cast off restraint.*" That means when you have a vision, it limits your choices; it restrains what you will do. So, a vision will keep you on track.

Jamie and I knew that God called us to the ministry. The Lord had spoken to me that it would grow and someday touch people around the world. And yet, what I was seeing and experiencing for the first ten years did not fit the vision I had on the inside of me. All the same, I was controlled by that vision.

That vision kept me from casting off restraint and perishing. At times, it just looked like what we were doing wasn't having a significant impact. But the vision of reaching people around the world kept me focused. It kept me going in a certain direction. It restrained my choices. I knew quitting wasn't an option.

You can actually get sidetracked if you aren't in relationship with God and if your vision isn't coming from Him. You can look at other people and think, *Why am I not prospering like them? Why aren't things working out for me the way they're working out for them?* But if you are secure with the vision God has given you, then it won't matter what anyone else is doing. That vision will restrain you from envy and covetousness.

Peter dealt with these things. After Jesus was resurrected and appeared to His disciples as they were fishing, He spoke to them about what was to come (John 21:1–23). And at one point (John 21:21), Peter referenced John and asked, "*What* shall *this man* do?"

Now, Jesus had already revealed something to Peter about His own future (John 21:18), and here he was asking about what would happen to "*the disciple whom Jesus loved*" (John 21:20–21). Jesus responded by saying that it was none of Peter's business.

You see, it's not good to compare ourselves among ourselves (2 Cor. 10:12). You need to be so single-minded (Phil. 3:13–15) in following the Lord that you don't look to the right or left to see what others are doing. It doesn't matter if you are doing what someone else is doing. The question is, are you doing all that the Lord has called you to do?

Chapter 15

Don't Limit God

Yea, they turned back and tempted God, and limited the Holy One of Israel.

Psalm 78:41

One of the most important encounters I've ever had with the Lord was on January 31, 2002. That's when God used Psalm 78:41 to show me that I was limiting Him through my small thinking.

We had struggled financially for decades, but we were getting to a place of relative comfort. We learned some things about financial prosperity in the mid-1990s, and the Lord opened the door for us to go on television in 2000. It seemed like we were finally seeing light at the end of the tunnel—and it wasn't another train!

All the same, I was still limiting God and not speaking the things He had shown me about having a worldwide ministry. Over the years, when I shared my vision with other people, they couldn't see it. They'd be nice and respond positively, but I knew they weren't receiving it.

In the early 1980s, my pastor, Dan Funkhouser, asked me what God had shown me about my life. I hadn't shared my vision with very many people. So, I told him the Lord had shown me that I would be ministering to people all over the world. At the time, people were staying away from our meetings by the thousands. And the way Pastor Dan tells it, he thought to himself, *Man, you're not hardly doing much right now. I don't know how this is going to play out.*

Pastor Dan and I are still friends today, and he even teaches at Charis, but it just goes to show how people evaluated my vision by what they were seeing. That's why it's important for you to use your imagination, which is the part of you that sees with your heart what you can't yet see with your physical eyes.

By 2002, though we had overcome financial difficulties and started a television program, I was limiting God. I knew where He wanted our ministry to go, and what His vision was, but I didn't see myself doing it. I wasn't using my imagination. Honestly, I was concerned that if I started seeing things the way God wanted me to, I would start trying to do things in my own strength, and it would negatively affect my relationship with Him. But the Lord spoke to me at the time and said, "I've spent thirty-four years working on you. You're going to have to trust me in this area."

I began to take the limits off God and started thinking big again. I began to think about what steps to take to see those things come to pass. At first, I didn't see anything with my physical eyes, but I did see things with my heart—in my imagination.

See with Your Heart

You have to be able to see things with your heart. The Word of God is not alive to many people because they read it with just their brains; they're only getting information. They don't take time to let the Word form a picture on the inside of them.

Years ago, I went to Israel as part of a tour. While we were there, many people were saying, "The Bible has just come alive to me!" They were crediting it to some special anointing on the land of Israel. But I don't believe that's so.

What actually happens is that people read the Bible, and they initially get facts and information. But when people go to the Holy Land, they see all of those places and things that they've read about in the Bible. And all of a sudden, the Bible "comes alive" because their imagination can finally picture things.

When I was in Israel, our bus went to the valley of Elah where David fought Goliath (1 Sam. 17:2). And there was nothing there. It hadn't been developed, so a person could see for miles. We stopped on the side of the road and the tour guide asked, "Does anybody want to get out?"

Because it was so hot outside, nobody wanted to get out of the bus except for me. I walked down to a little dry streambed and picked up five smooth stones just like David did (1 Sam. 17:40). I stood right where David was and looked where Goliath must have been, with the armies watching from both sides.

I was using my imagination. And because of that, the story of David killing Goliath (1 Sam. 17:48–51) came alive to me. It wasn't because of some special anointing on the Holy Land. It was because I saw it in my heart.

In our ministry, we've seen people raised from the dead. And I believe a big part of that was because I used my imagination. When I studied these instances in the Bible where people were raised from the dead, I didn't just read about them to get information. I took those stories and imagined myself taking part in them. I actually laid on a bed like Elisha did (2 Kgs. 4:34–35). I saw myself putting my hands on another person's hands and praying over them. I was imagining myself raising people from the dead.

You can't go anywhere in your physical body that you haven't already been in your imagination, so I knew I had to see these things in my heart first. When the time came that someone died and I commanded them to come back into their body, I already had a vision of myself raising people from the dead. In my imagination, I had already done these things in my heart. That opened the door to act on those things and see them come to pass in the physical realm.

Conceive the Vision

Years ago, when we were renovating our 110,000-square-foot building in Colorado Springs, I had our builder put tape on the floor to mark the places where every wall, door, or hallway would be, and I spent hours every night after everybody was gone, walking around that space. I wouldn't let myself step over the tape. In my imagination, I would see those walls.

I actually put five-gallon buckets on the floor and placed sheets of plywood on top of them to make a stage. I would stand on top of that platform and preach sermons in what would be our auditorium. In my imagination, I saw myself ministering to a room full of people. I know some of you think I'm weird for doing that, but I think you're weird not to use the imagination God has given you! And wouldn't you know, fourteen months later, that building was finished, and we moved in.

The Hebrew word *yetser* is translated *imagination* five different times in Scripture, including in Genesis 6:5:

> *And God saw that the wickedness of man* was *great in the earth, and* that *every imagination of the thoughts of his heart* was *only evil continually.*

The definition for *yetser* is "conception or purpose."[7] I believe that your imagination is where you conceive things. And just as a woman has to conceive a child in her physical body, you have to conceive miracles in your imagination. A stork doesn't deliver babies, nor do you go to the hospital and receive a baby. You have to conceive a baby and then give birth.

In 2009, when we purchased the property in Woodland Park that would become home to our Charis campus, it had just one building on it. It was 157 acres with a lodge. But as I prayed, God showed me all kinds of other buildings. Since then, we've built and acquired $150 million worth of assets there, including an additional piece of property where our ministry headquarters are.

I believe it all came about through the inspiration of the Holy Spirit. It came out of my relationship with the Lord. What I didn't know is that about the same time the Lord was speaking to me about starting Charis Bible College (in the early 1990s), the man who owned that property in Woodland Park got born again and dedicated it to Christian education.

As I was seeing the new college campus in my imagination, I saw windows all across the front of the buildings so students and visitors could look out at Pikes Peak. Later, I met the family of the former owner, and they told me the Lord had revealed a similar vision to their father just before he died—nearly twenty years before!

You see, those things weren't my ideas. Through my relationship with God, He placed the vision for all these Charis campus buildings in my heart. They were conceived in my imagination!

Principle VI

The Anointing

Chapter 16

Earn People's Respect

Let no man despise thy youth; but be thou an example of the believers, in word, in conversation, in charity, in spirit, in faith, in purity.

1 Timothy 4:12

If you are going to be a godly leader, people need to see that God's anointing is on you, the decisions you make, and the things you're doing. When I use the term "anointing" in this context, I'm talking about the manifest presence of God in what you are doing.

You can't just expect people to automatically respect you. They have to see that you are submitted to God and trusting in Him. In other words, you have a relationship with the Lord and are willing to do things His way. The anointing on your life is evidence of that.

In 1 Timothy, the Apostle Paul wrote to the church at Ephesus through Timothy. Paul is the one who started the church and put Timothy in charge of it. These people were born again under his ministry.

Paul could have come in and told these people, "I'm the apostle! Don't despise Timothy!" But instead of taking that approach, Paul told Timothy, "Don't let anybody despise your youth." Paul isn't telling the people to respect Timothy. He's telling Timothy, "Don't *you* let anybody disrespect you."

That's totally different than what many people would have done. There are some people who, if they think they're being discriminated against because they are part of a minority group, demand that others respect them. They demand that everybody else treat them a certain way. They're putting their problems on everyone and everything else. But you see, respect from other people has to be earned. The truth is that the only person holding you back in life is you!

My friend E.W. Jackson is a black man who was raised in a foster home for most of his childhood. By the time he was a teenager, he was spending his time on the streets. He was committing petty crimes as part of a gang. Thankfully, E.W.'s father stepped back into his life and provided him with structure and purpose. All the same, he could have spent the rest of his life just sitting there and crying about how he didn't have any opportunities because of the color of his skin.

Instead, E.W. joined the military, graduated with honors from Harvard, and became a successful lawyer. Then, after he was born again, he established a church, broadcast a daily radio program, and campaigned for public office—all without complaining about his circumstances. Today, Bishop E.W. Jackson is influencing his community and changing the world, all while giving glory to God.

Instead of demanding that people respect, honor, and follow you as a leader, you should earn people's respect. You should live in a way that honors the Lord. Then, they'll follow you because they see the power and anointing of God on you.

Seek Wisdom

> *And* [Rehoboam] *did evil, because he prepared not his heart to seek the Lord.*
>
> 2 Chronicles 12:14

The same Hebrew word that was translated "*prepared*" in this verse was also translated "established" (Prov. 16:3), "fixed" (Ps. 57:7), and "ordered" (Ps. 37:23).[8] It's talking about being so secure in your relationship with God and His anointing on your life that you won't be moved by anything else.

Rehoboam was a son of Solomon and inherited the throne when his father died (1 Kgs. 11:43). The people from the northern ten tribes of Israel came to Rehoboam and said that—through taxes and other things—"*Thy father made our yoke grievous*" (1 Kgs. 12:4).

They asked the new king to lighten the burden that was on them. In exchange, they would serve him faithfully. Rehoboam responded, "Give me three days to think it over." This was an important decision for the king and could have ensured unity among the tribes.

First, Rehoboam went to all the old men and sought their counsel. They said, if you will humble yourself and "*be a servant unto this people this day … they will be thy servants for ever*" (1 Kgs. 12:7). They at least encouraged the king to listen and consider the tribes' request. This was wisdom.

Then, Rehoboam went to the young men he grew up with. And they told him to say, "*My little* finger *shall be thicker than my father's loins,*" and "*My father hath chastised you with whips, but I will chastise you with scorpions*" (1 Kgs. 12:10–11). They encouraged Rehoboam to increase the burden on those ten tribes.

This is the way immaturity acts in leadership. Some people think they have to establish their authority by cracking the whip and saying, "I'm going to be even tougher than the last guy." That's the way the world system functions. They want to lead by intimidation and forcing people to do things. But Jesus said, "*He that is greatest among you shall be your servant*" (Matt. 23:11).

A characteristic of godly leadership is seeking wisdom. You need to be led by God in the decisions you make. It could be the difference in people accepting or rejecting your leadership. That's why the anointing on your life is so important. There needs to be a token of the Lord's manifest power in your life that causes people to respect you.

Rehoboam had an anointing on him as king. His father sought God for "*an understanding heart to judge*" His people (1 Kgs. 3:9). Rehoboam could have taken the same attitude and received wisdom (Prov. 4:7, James 1:5). But he wasn't established in the things of the Lord, and he was easily moved by the counsel of the young men. This resulted in the ten tribes following after someone else and the nation was divided (1 Kgs. 12:16–20).

For you to be a godly leader, people need to believe that you are hearing from God. They need to see that you are not just promoting yourself. It is important for people to see that the Lord is leading you.

Give Honor

> *Let the elders that rule well be counted worthy of double honour, especially they who labour in the word and doctrine.*
>
> 1 Timothy 5:17

There was a friend of mine who took over a church founded by another couple. They had pastored the church for more than twenty years, and then the husband died. The wife just didn't feel like she was supposed to continue pastoring, so she asked this friend of mine to step into the pulpit.

Typically, when there is a change of leadership, there are going to be people who don't like the new leader. They want things to stay the way they were. Now, my friend was young, and he was taking over from a pastor who had been older. So, in a sense, he was like Timothy taking over from Paul.

This looked like it would be a difficult situation. But this friend of mine used godly wisdom. He could have gone into that church and said, "I'm the new guy, and it's my way or the highway. I don't care what's happened before. This is how I'm going to do things." If he had done that, he would have offended all the people who loved the previous pastor. And that's a breeding ground for anything the devil wants to do (James 3:16).

Instead, this friend of mine took a certain portion of the foyer and dedicated it to the founding family. That's where he put pictures of them, the building, and other things explaining the history of the church. He honored the pastors by doing that.

Then, this man got up in front of the group and said, "I'm not going to be like the previous pastor. I'm a different person. God has put a different anointing on my life. But I'm standing on their shoulders." He made it clear that he had this opportunity because of what the previous pastors had done, and he wasn't going to tear down what they had built.

At the time, the previous pastors had several hundred members in their church. Within a few years of new leadership stepping in, attendance increased to over 2,000 people. They saw miraculous growth because the people who loved the previous pastors ended up loving the new guy for coming in and honoring them. He earned their respect, and they were willing to let their new pastor do things differently.

He also brought something new to the church. This blessed the people who were already there and brought in new people. He brought all these things together and the church more than doubled.

To be a godly leader, there's got to be an anointing on your life. People need to see you have a relationship with God and that you value things like honor. You can't just expect people to bow down to you and take your word that God put you in a position of leadership. You need to be able to demonstrate it.

Chapter 17

Show Some Proof

But I will come to you shortly, if the Lord will, and will know, not the speech of them which are puffed up, but the power. For the kingdom of God is *not in word, but in power.*

1 Corinthians 4:19–20

In the first four chapters of 1 Corinthians, Paul was defending the fact that he was an apostle. Some Christians were saying, "I *am of Paul,*" or "*I* am *of Apollos*" (1 Cor. 3:4), meaning they had set themselves apart according to the teachers they followed. There was division in the church.

Some even rejected Paul's leadership. He reasoned with them logically, but in these verses, he summed up his response by saying, "When I come, it's not going to be time for talk anymore. You either demonstrate that you are seeing people born again and that supernatural things are happening or sit down and shut up!"

He's telling these people that if they can't demonstrate the anointing of God on their lives, then they shouldn't be critical. It's the person who has the power working in their life who should be speaking.

I actually did this one time in the very early days of my ministry. Our Baptist Student Union set up a meeting in Clovis, New Mexico, where there was a college. A friend of mine and I were speaking about God doing miracles, but most of the people there didn't believe such things happened today. They barely believed in the miracles of the Bible!

They challenged us and claimed that Moses didn't cross the Red Sea. He crossed the "Reed Sea," which was more like a wetland and only six inches deep. They were saying, "See, it wasn't this great miracle, it was only six inches deep."

My friend who was with me had a great response to those things. He said, "Well, that means it was an even greater miracle than I thought." These people looked at him, puzzled for a moment. And then he said, "All of those Egyptians and their horses drowned in just six inches of water!"

The more we went on, the more contentious it got. People were yelling and telling us we were wrong. They were trying to tell us the way they represented God and tried to reach people was better than the way that we were doing it.

Finally, we told them, "Any person here who has led another person to the Lord in the last week can stand up and talk. But if you haven't led anybody to the Lord—if there's no fruit of God's power in your life—then sit down and shut up."

Not a single person out of a crowd of two hundred to three hundred people had witnessed to a person and led them to the Lord. So, we just grabbed our Bibles and walked out through the midst of them.

Confirm Your Calling

Years ago, I used to usher at Kathryn Kuhlman's meetings when I was still in the Baptist church. At the time, Kathryn Kuhlman had this huge healing ministry and saw great miracles happen. But, going into those meetings, I was skeptical of her.

I was brought up to be prejudiced against women being ministers. I was taught that they could minister to children, but not to adults. I'm not saying that's the way it should be. I'm just saying that's what I was told growing up in church.

Plus, Kathryn Kuhlman was just weird! She talked in an old style of English, saying things like "me thinks" instead of "I think." She also wore long, flowing gowns with big sleeves, and she moved around like she was floating across the stage. It was quite a show! So, there were a lot of things about her that turned me off as a good Baptist boy. But I still wanted to be an usher in that service so I could see what all the excitement was about.

Because a lot of supernatural healings took place in Kathryn Kuhlman's ministry, a lot of really sick people came to her meetings. People would come in wheelchairs and stretchers, but because of fire codes, they couldn't just be in the aisles between the seats.

As an usher, I had to take one woman off a stretcher and put her in a chair. This woman couldn't have weighed sixty pounds and looked just like the people you'd see in pictures of concentration camps in World War II. She was nearly dead.

After I got through completing the preliminary things for the meeting, I went and sat on the floor right in front of the stage while Kathryn Kuhlman ministered. I was only five or six feet away, and, like I said, it seemed like everything she did was weird. It just didn't bless me.

Then, at the invitation, I saw a woman come running to the front of the auditorium. It was the one who I'd taken off the stretcher and put in a chair! Before, she had been so frail and weak. But here she was pushing her stretcher down the aisle, jumping up on the stage, and totally healed.

Through that experience, I saw the anointing of God on Kathryn Kuhlman's ministry. And the moment I saw that anointing working through her, all of my prejudices about women in ministry left. It didn't matter if I thought she was acting weird and talking in a strange accent. I saw the anointing of God on her, and I immediately acknowledged that God had put her in a position of leadership.

I couldn't deny there was an anointing there because things were happening that could not be explained without God. That's because, for a person to be a godly leader, there needs to be some manifestation of God's presence and power in their life.

Build Trust

> *And God wrought special miracles by the hands of Paul: so that from his body were brought unto the sick handkerchiefs or aprons, and the diseases departed from them, and the evil spirits went out of them.*
>
> Acts 19:11–12

Why should someone believe your opinions more than their own? You can't just tell people, "God has anointed me," "God made me an apostle," or "God made me a prophet." No, there must be some demonstration of the power of God in your life.

The Apostle Paul defended his position because he had demonstrated in word and power. There was proof of the anointing on his ministry, so much so that people took pieces of cloth off him and saw miracles happen!

Once, some of my staff ministered with me at an event, and some attendees weren't showing them the same respect shown to me. Now, I don't think that's right. But on the other hand, I told them, "It takes time to build people's trust."

There are people who have followed me *for years*. They've seen the fruit of my ministry. They have heard stories about people being raised from the dead, healed, and delivered. Because of that, they show me a degree of respect. They receive from me in a way they may not from someone they haven't seen demonstrate an anointing.

In the early days of this ministry, we saw miraculous things happen. But we started by ministering to just a few people. It was over time that our influence grew. And that took decades! It happened so gradually that it was hard to comprehend.

Back in 2002, I was interviewed on the radio by Len and Cathy Mink. Right before I went into the studio, I heard Len talking about how I was one of the ministers he listened to on the radio right after he got born again. Here was a guy who was ministering to thousands of people on radio, and on stage with Kenneth Copeland, and yet he said I had influenced his life.

When he said that, I was shocked. I was just so focused on doing what God called me to do, I hadn't stopped to really think about who I was influencing—*even after twenty-five years of broadcasting on radio!* But it was the anointing on my life that was making an impact.

I remember a speaker at our Bible college who was making a point and said, "I don't have time to explain this. Just trust me." He was a young guy who had been in ministry for less than a year. So, my first thought was, *Why should I trust you?*

I'm not condemning anyone, but I put a lot of value on a person's experience. Anyone can start strong, but I really admire people who have been at things for a long time and are still successful. I've seen the proof in their lives and ministries that they are doing what God called them to do.

Chapter 18

Release the Power

Despise not prophesyings. Prove all things; hold fast that which is good.

1 Thessalonians 5:20-21

I remember one instance when I was ministering in a church in Wales. It was an old stone structure that seated about a hundred people. That night, there were only about forty or fifty people there, and only three or four of them were younger than sixty. Most of them were seventy or eighty years old.

Some people were using walkers, some of them were in wheelchairs, and many of them were falling asleep as I was ministering. They weren't receiving anything, so I just stopped. I was only five minutes into my message, and nobody was listening.

I said, "We're going to pray and see the power of God manifest." And when I started praying, God gave me a word. There was a woman sitting on the front row with three kids. One of them was a teenager and the others were younger. They were the only young people in the whole church. God showed me something about this woman and I started speaking to her.

I said, "You've been grieving over something. I don't know what it is, but you have been in grief." And when I said that, all those older people in the church woke up and started paying attention. So, I went on and prophesied to this woman. I said, "This was the devil," along with some other things.

All of a sudden, we started seeing people healed, coming out of wheelchairs, and throwing their crutches down. We had all kinds of miracles happen in that little church where, before, people were nodding off and not receiving my ministry.

After the whole thing was over, I found out that the woman on the front row was the previous pastor's wife. The pastor had died, and then one of her children died. The kids with her were her grandchildren. And here she was, just grieving and in a terrible situation.

Now, I didn't know any of those things before I started sharing a word with that woman. But because I flowed in the gifts of the Holy Spirit and said things that I couldn't know on my own, it grabbed people's attention.

One of the older ladies later told me that this particular church was where Smith Wigglesworth ministered when he came to the area. Back in the early twentieth century, all kinds of miracles manifested through that man's ministry. So much so, that he is still widely revered by Christians today.

This lady said they saw miraculous things happen when Smith Wigglesworth preached. So, when I started operating in the supernatural, they recognized God speaking through me. I believed what I was ministering was good, but those people had gotten used to not seeing anything supernatural happen. To get them to pay attention and receive what the Lord wanted me to share, I had to demonstrate the anointing of God.

God Will Confirm

> *And Elijah came unto all the people, and said, How long halt ye between two opinions? if the Lord* be *God, follow him: but if Baal,* then *follow him. And the people answered him not a word.*
>
> 1 Kings 18:21

To be a godly leader, you have to show proof of the anointing of God on your life. And in a sense, this is exactly what Elijah did in the Old Testament when he challenged the prophets of Baal and the prophets of the groves who had turned the people away from worshipping the one true God (1 Kgs. 18:19–20).

Elijah said, "Let's have a contest!" He told the false prophets to place a sacrifice on an altar but not put any fire on it. Elijah would do the same with his sacrifice. Then, they would pray and see if Baal or the God of Israel would answer by fire.

In other words, the side that could manifest the presence, or demonstrate an anointing, would reveal the true God. Elijah was saying, "Let's see who actually responds in power, and let that be the one we worship."

So, the prophets of Baal went from morning until night. They even cut themselves and jumped on the altar as if they were willing to be a sacrifice themselves, asking their god to send fire (1 Kgs. 18:26–28). But nothing happened. Elijah actually mocked them and said, "Maybe he's asleep. Maybe he's on a journey. You need to cry louder" (1 Kgs. 18:27). I just love that attitude!

After the false prophets were finished, Elijah prepared his sacrifice and had the sacrifice, wood, and altar drenched with water. Then, he prayed a really simple prayer and said, "*Let it be known this day that thou* art *God in Israel, and* that *I* am *thy servant, and* that *I have done all these things at thy word*" (1 Kgs. 18:36). You see, Elijah didn't just come up with a plan and do these things himself. No, God spoke to him.

The Lord told Elijah what he was supposed to do. And because of it, fire fell from heaven. It not only consumed the sacrifice but also the wood and the water in the trench around the altar. It just consumed everything. When they saw these things, the people fell on their faces and said, "*The* L*ORD*, *he* is *the God*" (1 Kgs. 18:39).

For you to be a leader, you need to have God confirm His Word with signs following (Mark 16:20). You need to have a manifest presence of God in your life. And there are no shortcuts. You can't compromise and get there.

If you are in relationship with God, He will confirm what He is doing through you. He's not going to confirm *your* will or *your* plans. The Lord will only confirm the things that He has conceived on the inside of you.

Signs Will Follow

> *And they went forth, and preached every where, the Lord working with* them, *and confirming the word with signs following. Amen.*
>
> Mark 16:20

God is with us constantly. He'll never leave us nor forsake us (Heb. 13:5). There's nowhere that we can go to escape from God (Ps. 139:8–10). These things are true in the spirit. But the anointing is the *manifest* presence of God.

I believe this is why the Lord told His disciples that signs would follow those who believe on Him (Mark 16:17–20). Jesus used miracles like a dinner bell to draw people. And if you're going to be a godly leader, you need to be able to manifest, or display, the presence and power of God in your life. And it's not just limited to ministry.

If you are in business or some other area, God wants to manifest Himself because you have an area of influence. The anointing on you will cause you to prosper in whatever things you put your hand to (Deut. 28:8). And that will get people's attention!

In the early years of our ministry, I once worked in a photography studio to pay back the rent we owed to our landlord. The landlord owned the studio and said he needed help developing photographs. I didn't know anything about photography, but I knew the Lord and had been baptized in the Holy Spirit. So, I decided the best thing to do was pray in tongues while I worked and get wisdom on how to do it.

Well, the Lord showed me some things. It wasn't long before I was developing photos to such a degree that even the owner said he couldn't replicate what I was doing. He was so impressed that he eventually offered me a 50 percent stake in his business. And it was all because the presence of God manifested through the anointing that was on me.

Colin Carr is on our board of directors and is a Charis graduate. He and his wife April believed the Lord was leading them to start their own business, so they sought my advice. After they explained everything, I said, "That sounds like God to me!" So, I agreed with them in prayer, and they started in the healthcare real estate business. Colin and April's testimony is that they followed the wisdom of the Lord in everything they did.

Their decisions and the exponential growth they experienced in just a short time showed that God was working supernaturally through them. Today, their company is worth millions of dollars, and they have offices all around the country. An anointing for business manifested in their lives and influenced people around them, which led to miraculous healings and other things.

There was a supernatural, manifest presence of God on the early apostles. And that's one of the reasons people followed them. If God worked supernaturally through believers in the early Church, why should we be any different today as godly leaders?

Principle VII

Patience

Chapter 19

Wait on the Lord

Wait on the Lord: be of good courage, and he shall strengthen thine heart: wait, I say, on the Lord.

Psalm 27:14

Many people believe that patience is just sitting around and doing nothing. They think you're waiting on God the way that you would wait on a bus—just wasting time. That is not what the Scripture describes as patience.

When the Bible talks about waiting on the Lord (Ps. 27:14), it's similar to the way a waiter waits on a person at a restaurant. It's an active thing, not passive. A good waiter will be watching the diners at their table, and when their glasses begin to get empty, they'll come over and offer a refill. When a person is ready for their check, all they have to do is look at the waiter, and it will be brought to their table.

That's the way that patience is. It isn't just being passive and not doing anything. A person shouldn't lie on their couch, watching television, goofing off all day, and saying, "I'm just waiting on the Lord." No! Waiting is active patience.

When Moses spent forty years in the wilderness (Acts 7:30), he endured patiently because he had a vision of what God was going to do in his life (Heb. 11:27). When the Bible talks about enduring, it doesn't mean just putting up with things. Moses was persevering. Perseverance is another way of saying waiting.

I believe that patience is just faith over a prolonged period of time. That's in contrast to having a momentary burst of faith. You can go into a ministry meeting, hear the Word of God, see some miracles happen, and your faith can peak.

Faith can rise to a crescendo in a moment, and people can get hooked on that. That's why some people follow certain ministers around, going from meeting to meeting and conference to conference. But patience goes beyond where you just occasionally come to a place of believing God.

The Apostle Paul wrote "*The just shall live by faith*" (Rom. 1:17). You have to *live* in the realm of faith, which is patience. And as I've grown in my relationship with the Lord, I'm operating in more patience. I'm not saying I've arrived in this area, but I've certainly left. I'm much more patient than I used to be. And I've actually gotten to where time is my friend.

Don't Be Pressured

Back in 2009, when we were considering purchasing the property that became the site of our main Charis campus, I went to look at it with some of my staff.

It was originally listed at $16 million for 157 acres, and it had a lodge on it that was worth between $3 million and $4 million. But that was *before* the Great Recession. As a result, the people who owned the property just needed to get it off their hands. By the time we looked at it, they had lowered the total price to $4 million.

As we stood on the lodge balcony, I asked my staff for their thoughts. We all believed buying the property was what God wanted us to do. So, we told the real estate agent that we would pray about it.

That's when he said, "Well, you've got to put in an offer today. We've already got another offer on this property—a cash offer. If you don't make an offer today, you're going to lose it!" I've since learned this is a ploy some real estate agents use to pressure buyers. I don't know if that was true in this case or not. But we were being compelled to make a decision on the spot.

I just told this guy, "I'm not going to make a decision right now. I think this is what we're going to do, but I'm going to take some time and pray about it. If this is what God has for me, it'll be there when I get through praying about it. I'm not going to be forced into doing something."

That real estate agent just couldn't understand why I would do that. He knew we wanted this property and thought we would make an offer on the spot. After he left, a member of my executive team came to me and said, "Now I know that this is of God, because you aren't acting under pressure." He saw that I wasn't going to do something in the flesh. I was going to pray about it, and I was at peace. In other words, he recognized that I was operating in patience.

That is one of the ways you can tell if God is leading you. If you are under pressure to do something, God is probably not leading you. When you flow with God and follow His leadership, patience will be present in your life.

Hope Deferred

> *Hope deferred maketh the heart sick: but when the desire cometh,* it is *a tree of life.*
>
> Proverbs 13:12

I don't set five- and ten-year goals. I rarely place a time limit on things. I just have a relationship with God. And when He speaks to me and shows me what to do, I do it. That way, I'm not under pressure to make decisions.

Proverbs 13:12 says that if you put your hope in something and put a time limit on seeing it manifest, you're setting yourself up for disappointment. For example, if you believe that God is going to heal you, supply a need, turn your relationship around, or prosper your business, and you put a deadline on it, you're setting yourself up to be heartsick.

My approach is to find out what God wants me to do and determine to get it done. I don't know if it will take a year, five years, or ten years, but I will get done what God tells me to do. I've just learned to have patience.

In 2003, when we purchased that 110,000-square-foot facility in Colorado Springs, we needed another $3.2 million to renovate the building for our ministry and Bible school. The Lord told me to do it without a loan, I committed myself to that, and our partners supplied the funds we needed.

We wanted to move in by September 2004, but we didn't do so until November of that year, two months later than our original plan. At the opening rally, a woman came up to me and asked, "Are you disappointed that you missed your deadline?" And I just kind of laughed and said, "No, I'm not disappointed."

I told this woman that I had just experienced the greatest miracle of financial provision I had seen in my life (up to that point). We saw $3.2 million come into the ministry in fourteen months. And that building was finished debt free! I went on to say, "We got this thing done! I would have liked to move in earlier, but I've never done anything perfectly in my life."

Now, I will admit that when the Lord spoke to me about launching our Gospel Truth Network, I felt like there was a sense of urgency to get it done sooner rather than later. So, I told my staff that we needed to be ready by the end of summer 2024. But I believed that was from the Lord.

In response, my staff went above and beyond. They created more new shows than we originally envisioned, making it possible to provide original programming twenty-four hours a day, seven days a week. Everything was done with excellence.

Nevertheless, if we don't get something done by a certain time, I'm not going to fall apart. I'm still going to rejoice. I'm not going to let my heart be sick.

Chapter 20

Gain Experience

Thou therefore endure hardness, as a good soldier of Jesus Christ.

2 Timothy 2:3

When I was drafted into the military and sent to Vietnam, they taught us how to shoot a weapon. They taught us how to throw hand grenades. They taught us how to be soldiers. But it was just book learning. They didn't teach us to have patience.

When soldiers first got to Vietnam, they were dangerous. That's because they thought they knew what they were doing, even though they had no practical experience. The people who had been in Vietnam for a while not only had the training, but they had also learned to "*endure hardness.*" That experience just took them to another level as soldiers. When we got in combat, we didn't rely on new soldiers in ways we relied upon seasoned soldiers.

I remember sitting with other soldiers on bunker guard duty one night, eating our C-rations, and we had a new guy with us. It was his first day in the field, so he was still pretty green. Our base was out in the middle of the fighting, so gunfire and explosions happened all the time. Because of that, we could shoot our weapons or throw a grenade any time we wanted.

This new guy was excited. He asked, "Can I shoot my weapon anytime I want?" And we said, "Sure!" So, he took his M16 and shot it down the hill. Then he asked, "Can I throw a hand grenade?" And we said, "You can do it anytime you want to."

We had hundreds of hand grenades in that bunker. So, this guy took one and tried pulling the pin, but he made a classic mistake. Those pins would sometimes get stuck. He pulled it really hard, and when he did, the grenade fell out of his hand. I was sitting on a big rock, eating my C-rations at the time, and that grenade rolled right between my feet!

When I saw it, I went over backward, threw my food in the air, and hid behind that rock to avoid the explosion. But it never went off. You see, we were trained with "pineapple" grenades from the Korean War, and they didn't have a safety on them. But the newer "baseball" grenades were smaller, had more shrapnel in them, and had a safety.

This guy had forgotten to take the safety off. So, even though he pulled the pin, the safety was still on. But we didn't know that! Thankfully, when it didn't go off, we just took the safety off and threw it down the hill.

If this guy had some experience, he likely wouldn't have jumped at the chance to shoot his rifle and throw hand grenades. He may have exercised more patience and not put lives at risk unnecessarily.

The Word Builds Patience

> *For whatsoever things were written aforetime were written for our learning, that we through patience and comfort of the scriptures might have hope.*
>
> Romans 15:4

People like that new guy in Vietnam are dangerous because they think they know what they're doing, but they have no practical experience. Because he hadn't thrown a grenade like that before, he lost control of it. We all could have been hurt. So, we gave a wide berth to people like that.

Training alone is not going to make you a good soldier. You have to apply that training. And once you go through a firefight—and live through it—you're going to be a better soldier than someone who only has book knowledge.

This is one of the reasons why so many soldiers in Vietnam did not respect lieutenants who were new in the field. It's because these new officers had come straight out of school. They had authority but no practical experience. They were trying to do everything by the book, which didn't work in guerrilla warfare.

Being patient enough to know what to do and when to do it could be the difference between life and death. Someone with practical experience will take time to evaluate things and make a wise decision.

Like an officer on the battlefield, a godly leader has to exercise patience. For example, someone may show you a great idea that could help your business or church. But if you've been in the field and gained some experience, you'll evaluate those things differently than someone who is green and "gung-ho" about everything. That patience may keep you from making a monumental mistake.

Having battlefield experience is important, but that also doesn't mean a person should go out to the enemy, embrace them, and say, "Thank you for making me better!" No, the enemy is sent to kill you! But if you use what you've been trained to do and put it into practice, you will gain experience. And that *experience* will make you a better soldier.

Likewise, your enemy, the devil, is not sent by God to give you patience. But when the enemy comes, if you apply the Word and trust God, you will develop patience as a result.

When you come into tribulation, if you apply what God has taught you, you will gain experience. And you'll be stronger and better off than you were before. It comes through the Scripture, but you have to put it to work. You have to prove your faith.

Patience is faith that has been proven. It's been exercised, like muscles. All of us have the same muscles, but not all of us look the same because we haven't developed them. We haven't put them to use. If you are going to be a godly leader, you're going to have to exercise patience.

Growth Takes Time

> *For the earth bringeth forth fruit of herself; first the blade, then the ear, after that the full corn in the ear.*
>
> Mark 4:28

What God has called you to do will not come to pass automatically. Things will come in steps and stages, which will require you to use patience. If you must have things right away, other people will manipulate and pressure you into doing things contrary to God's Word. If you do that, you will wind up crashing and burning.

There was once a couple who were students at our school, and they saw the prosperity operating in my life. They thought, *If the Lord can do that for Andrew, He'll do that for us!* While it is true that "*God is no respecter of persons*" (Acts 10:34), it took me *decades* of going through steps and stages to reach that point.

This couple just wanted to skip all that growth and go straight to being prosperous. So, they rented a huge house for $5,500 a month when the average rent for a home was around $1,000. And it wasn't long before they got into a bind thinking God would just take care of things.

Now, I'm not condemning anyone, and you should trust the Lord to be your source. But this couple thought it would be easy to trust God for a $5,500 house payment despite not having believed God for anything before! They wanted to go directly from sowing a seed to receiving a harvest.

As the old saying goes, "How do you eat an elephant? One bite at a time." And over the years, the Lord has shown me that I need to do things in bite-sized pieces according to what my faith can handle at the moment.

Years ago, I got determined about a project that would have been bigger than anything we had done before. I believed it was the Lord's direction to implement it all at once. But our board of directors advised me to do it in stages because of the financial strain it could cause. When I made it clear that we should just move forward with the whole project, those men came to me and said, "If you believe this is the Lord, we won't stand in your way. But we will give our resignations."

You see, they could not support what I wanted to do in good conscience. And when they did that, it caused me to take a step back and re-evaluate things. As it turned out, if we had gone ahead all at once, it would have jeopardized the ministry. So, we just took things one step at a time. Praise the Lord for godly board members who loved me enough to tell me the truth.

God may not be giving you more responsibility right now because you're not ready. But you can take steps toward it. There is first a blade, then the ear, then the full corn in the ear. You need to exercise patience.

Chapter 21

Keep Standing

But let patience have her *perfect work, that ye may be perfect and entire, wanting nothing.*

James 1:4

Patience is a godly trait. It is also a sign of maturity. You need to learn to operate in patience if you plan to be a mature and godly leader.

God told Abraham that He would make of him a great nation (Gen. 12:1–4) and that he would be the father of many nations (Gen. 17:4). This was at least twenty-six years before Isaac was born (Gen. 21:5). For twenty-six years, Abraham was patient, waiting on God's promise. Then, twenty-two years after that, Abraham offered Isaac as a sacrifice before the Lord stopped him (Gen. 22:1–12). That was nearly fifty years of walking with the Lord and trusting Him.

For many people in the Bible, it took time for God's calling to manifest. With Moses, there were forty years in the wilderness (Acts 7:30) followed by another forty years of leading the children of Israel into the Promised Land.

With David, there were thirteen years from the time he was anointed (1 Sam. 16:12–13) until he started seeing the will of God come to pass, followed by another forty years of being king—a total of fifty-three years.

After his salvation, the Apostle Paul spent three and a half years in the deserts of Arabia before starting his ministry (Gal. 1:17–18). It just takes time to grow in the Lord. But if you say, "Unless God does something in this amount of time, I'm going to quit," then you are not letting "*patience have her perfect work.*"

I had a woman come to me with a tooth problem. She attended one of my meetings on a Saturday night and had a dentist's appointment scheduled for the following Monday. This woman was experiencing severe pain and wanted to be healed without having to go to the dentist. She just wanted to receive directly from God.

This woman told me, "If I'm not healed by Monday morning, then I'm going to the dentist and get it taken care of that way." So, I prayed with her right then. But she was still in pain that night. The pain didn't leave on Sunday either.

On Monday morning, it was getting down to crunch time. Either she had to get ready to go to the dentist, or she was just going to have to stand and believe God. Finally, she said, "I don't care how long it takes, but I'm believing God." So, she called and canceled her dentist appointment. Within twenty or thirty minutes, the pain was totally gone, and she was healed of that toothache. She just kept standing for her healing until it manifested.

To be a godly leader, you need to be patient, and when you think you've done all to stand, keep standing (Eph. 6:13).

Life Is Not a Sprint

> *And we desire that every one of you do shew the same diligence to the full assurance of hope unto the end: that ye be not slothful, but followers of them who through faith and patience inherit the promises.*
>
> Hebrews 6:11–12

These verses precede the ones about the faith Abraham demonstrated while waiting for God's promises to come to pass (Heb. 6:13–15). At any point during those years, Abraham could have said, "That's it. This isn't working. I quit!" And in a sense, by conceiving Ishmael with Hagar, some may say he did. But the Scripture says Abraham "*patiently endured*" and "*obtained the promise*" (Heb. 6:15).

As long as you set a deadline on something, Satan knows it's unlikely that you will stand and believe God over the long haul. So, he's going to push you and try to get you to quit. He'll fight you right up to the last second. But the moment he sees that quitting is no longer an option for you and that it doesn't matter how long it takes, you'll see things come to pass.

I believe you'll actually speed up the manifestation of the thing you're believing for when you get that kind of attitude. You just need to have a mindset that no matter how long something takes, you're going to stand and believe God.

Many people only believe in God for short bursts, like a sprinter. They will do a devotional or a Bible study, and for the next thirty minutes, they'll keep their mind stayed on the Lord (Is. 26:3) to meet a need. They might operate in faith in that moment, but then over the rest of their day, they'll just push God aside.

They'll do their own thing and then wonder why the things of God aren't operating consistently. It's because their faith is flagging. They are not living by faith.

Faith can be momentary, but life is a marathon and not a sprint. Again, patience is just faith over a prolonged period of time. We can't believe for a moment and then fall away to unbelief when circumstances go against us. We have to believe and then continue in faith (have patience) until the desired end comes.

If you can get to where your faith is consistent instead of just operating in short bursts, that's when you see everything perfect and complete (James 1:4). You have to use your faith at times other than on Sundays when you go to church. You have to get to where you are *living* by faith (Heb. 10:38), and that's what patience really is.

Remember Victories

I remember an instance involving one of the managers of our ministry who had been a banker. He had been the president of a bank, and I thought that having handled large amounts of money would make him a good fit for us. But it didn't turn out that way.

When this man came into my ministry, our income was fluctuating month to month. It would be way down during some months and way up in other months. My partners would sometimes give and sometimes not give, and our income just fluctuated dramatically.

This guy was used to running a bank. He was used to consistent revenue coming in. And here we were, not really knowing one month to the next how much money would come in. Praise the Lord, that's changed! But at the time, it was all over the place. And this guy just panicked!

He came to me one month and said, "Do you realize that we've got more expenses this month than income?" And I said, "Yes, I understand that." The next month, he came to me again and said, "We still have more expenses than we've got income." And I said, "I hear you."

Then, the month after that, this man came to me and said, "You aren't listening! This is the third month in a row that our income is less than our expenses!" He was panicking and said, "You've got to do something!"

Now, I could have reacted like he did, but I used patience instead. Because of experiences that we'd had throughout our lives and ministry, I knew it just wasn't that big of a deal. I had gotten used to exercising faith over a long period of time. And because of it, we persevered.

One time, we were having a board meeting at my house. Our income was very small; probably less than a million dollars a year. And on paper, we were broke. Our board said, "You are bankrupt. We're going to close the ministry down."

I didn't believe it was what God wanted, but I didn't really have much of an argument to make. So, I said, "Well, let's pray." And while we were praying, the phone rang. On the other end was my mother, who was opening the mail for our ministry. She said, "We just got a $60,000 check!" It was an offering from a church that I'd never been to before or since. And it covered all of our shortfall!

When things like that happen, it produces a positive experience. So, when we were having financial problems, I had a different perspective than my manager did. He was just seeing the worst-case scenario in the short term. But once you put the Word of God into effect and you've seen the Lord come through time after time, it gives you confidence. You're emboldened to stand and keep going over the long haul. It builds your faith and produces patience.

Principle VIII

Don’t Quit

Chapter 22

Supernatural Strength

[Charity] *beareth all things, believeth all things, hopeth all things, endureth all things. Charity never faileth.*

1 Corinthians 13:7–8a

Something that goes along with being patient is not quitting. And that goes back to your relationship with the Lord. Because God doesn't have any quit in Him, if you are truly in fellowship with Him, there shouldn't be any quit in you either.

God is never bummed out. The Lord is never wringing His hands, thinking, *There's no way I can solve this problem.* So, if you feel like you just can't take it anymore and you're ready to quit, that's an indication that you aren't really in fellowship with the Lord. You're more focused on the problem than you are on the problem solver.

In these verses, when the Apostle Paul is talking about "*charity,*" he's talking about the characteristics of God's kind of love. It bears all things, believes all things, hopes all things, and endures all things. God's kind of love never fails.

That means if you say, "I just can't bear any more of this," you are actually saying that God's kind of love is not working in you. God's kind of love can bear anything. If you don't believe that things will work and you've lost hope, you aren't operating in God's kind of love. You're operating out of your own flesh.

If you aren't plugged into the Lord, you aren't drawing on His power. But if you are really in relationship with God, He infuses you with the kind of love that bears all things, believes all things, hopes all things, endures all things, and never fails. That's because the Holy Spirit gives you supernatural strength to overcome.

The spirit of the Lord came upon Samson, and he would perform all these feats of strength like carrying away the city gates. If you ever see movies about Samson, they portray him as a big guy who looks like a bodybuilder. But if you read the Bible, it says that people wanted to know what his secret was.

If Samson had been this massive hunk of muscle, nobody would have wondered what his secret was. It's more likely that he had an average physical build, but he could do these supernatural things. There was an anointing on his life that enabled him to do it.

If what you are doing is truly ordained of God—meaning, you heard from the Lord and you're just obeying Him—you will be infused with supernatural strength. For example, when David was a young shepherd, I believe an anointing came on him when he killed the lion and the bear with his bare hands. (1 Sam. 17:34–36).

Some people may think he used a sling, like he did with Goliath. But the Scripture says he took a lion by the beard. How could a teenager overpower and kill a lion? It was the spirit of might that came upon him.

A Spirit of Might

> *He giveth power to the faint; and to* them that have *no might he increaseth strength.*
>
> Isaiah 40:29

Through a spirit of might, you can do things you wouldn't be able to do in your own strength. I've had things happen to me that I look back on and think, *How in the world did I ever do that?* But it was because I was in communion with God and His presence manifested in my life.

The Bible says, "*as thy days,* so shall *thy strength* be" (Deut. 33:25). If you come into a crisis situation, the Lord will just anoint you. If you are really in fellowship with God the way you should be, there won't be any quit in you. That's because the Holy Spirit will rise when things seem hopeless, and you will have a supernatural ability to respond.

A person who is burned out and ready to give up isn't plugged into the Lord. There is no lack of power in God. As Christians, that power is available to us, but we aren't drawing on it. For example, I've heard that 80 percent of all people who enter the ministry quit within five years.[9] And of the 20 percent who stay, 80 percent are nearing burnout.[10]

That means only 4 percent of ministers last more than five years and are still thriving, instead of just surviving. That's a terrible statistic, but I can believe it's true. I've seen countless ministers come and go and others struggle just to keep their noses above water.

It's not because they aren't doing good things. It's that they are doing those things in their own strength. They're trying to meet the needs of people out of their own strength and ability. One of the tricks of Satan is to get people so busy doing ministry that they don't have time for God.

Since 1968, when the Lord touched my life, it's been rare that I've gone a day without getting in the Word of God and spending time in fellowship with the Lord. Recently, more demands have been put on me because of our television network. My recording schedule has tripled, which means I'm busier than ever. At some point, I realized that I'd gone two days without opening my Bible except to minister the Word. That's not healthy!

I had to tell my staff that we needed to slow down. They were shocked, but I had to put my relationship with God first. I need to fellowship with Him on a daily basis. And I really believe that's why I have kept going strong all these years. There's nothing special about me. I just recognize that I can do nothing without God and His strength.

The Need for Rest

> *And he said unto them, Come ye yourselves apart into a desert place, and rest a while: for there were many coming and going, and they had no leisure so much as to eat.*
>
> Mark 6:31

God never intended the ministry to be tough on people. If you think about it, most people would never take a job where they're on call twenty-four hours a day. And yet, I can name many ministers who haven't taken a vacation in years.

They work all day long, serving people. Then, they wake up in the middle of the night to take a phone call from someone seeking ministry. They just have to be available all of the time. And it's a good desire to minister to people, but they aren't putting limits on themselves.

Remember, pastors are a gift from God to the church (Eph. 4:11–13). But that's not always the way people treat them. I heard about a pastor who hadn't taken a vacation in seven years. He had scheduled a week off, loaded his family in the car, and as he was locking the front door, he heard the phone ring.

His wife told him not to answer it. This was in the days before mobile phones, so he could have just left, and nobody would have been able to contact him. But this pastor said, "I've got to answer it because it could be urgent!" As it turned out, the chairman of the deacons' board had died and it was the church calling to say, "Pastor, we need you." So, this man canceled his family vacation and stayed to minister to the people.

Sometime later, I was speaking to a ministers' group in Colorado Springs about the need to rest. I told them they had to put limits on themselves as leaders and take time off. I used the example of Jesus, who called His disciples apart into a desert place to rest for a while (Mark 6:31–32).

After hearing those things, the minister who had canceled his family vacation returned to his church and told them, "From now on, Monday is my day off. I don't care what's happening. I don't care if someone dies! I am not available. You can call somebody else in the church."

As you can imagine, that caused no small stir. Afterward, a woman came up to this man and said, "Pastor, the devil never takes a day off." So, he responded, "Well, if I don't take a day off, I'm going to be just like the devil!"

You see, a leader can only run on an empty tank for so long. You can't give from what you don't have. If you don't take time to rest and draw on your relationship with the Lord, you'll get frustrated, burned out, and be tempted to quit. But like God, a godly leader doesn't have any quit in them.

Chapter 23

Just Keep Going

And straightway Jesus constrained his disciples to get into a ship, and to go before him unto the other side, while he sent the multitudes away.

Matthew 14:22

As I've said, one of the most important moments in my ministry was when the Lord spoke to me through Psalm 78:41 and showed me I was limiting Him through my small thinking. And one of the key things in that verse was that the children of Israel "*turned back*" when God called them into the Promised Land. I've learned that when God tells you to go in a certain direction, you shouldn't turn back.

When Jesus told His disciples to get into the boat and go to the other side of the Sea of Galilee, He sent them away and then went up into a mountain to pray. While the disciples were out there in the boat, they came into a terrible storm (Matt. 14:22–33).

Now, it's only a two-hour trip from one side of the Sea of Galilee to the other. But here they were in the fourth watch of the night, between 3 a.m. and 6 a.m., still trying to cross. Remember, they left before it was dark. So, nine hours later, they were only halfway across when it should have been just a two-hour trip. That means the wind was blowing against them.

As you read the story, you'll see that they experienced a miracle when Jesus walked on water to them. Then Peter got out of the boat and walked on water to go to Jesus. When Jesus and Peter got back into the boat, not only did the wind cease, but immediately the boat was translated to the other side of the lake (John 6:21). So, there were a lot of miracles happening, one right after the other.

Everybody would love to experience miracles like that, but all those things started when God told them to get into the boat and go to the other side. He didn't say to go halfway and drown! But He also didn't say, "If there's no opposition, then go to the other side." That's really important.

Remember, they had the wind blowing against them. If they were going to try and preserve their own lives, all they had to do was turn that boat around and head back for the shore they just came from. And with the wind blowing that much, they could have been there in just a few minutes. But to their credit, they didn't turn around.

When a two-hour trip turned into nine hours, and they were only halfway across, they were at least headed in the direction that God sent them. Even though everything was against them, they were still doing what the Lord told them to do. If you want to see the miraculous power of God in your life as a leader, one of the keys is that you've got to get started and then not turn back.

Stay Committed

> *And after he had seen the vision, immediately we endeavoured to go into Macedonia, assuredly gathering that the Lord had called us for to preach the gospel unto them.*
>
> Acts 16:10

The Apostle Paul had made plans to go into Asia and then Bithynia, but the Holy Spirit forbade him. Then, in the middle of the night, the Lord gave Paul a vision of where he was to go next (Acts 16:6–10).

I believe the Lord communicated something in a dream because, if He didn't get Paul while he was asleep, he would have started going in yet another direction. You see, Paul didn't assume that he was sitting at a red light, waiting on a green light from God to move forward. In his mind, Paul already had a green light from the Lord—"*Go ye into all the world, and preach the gospel*" (Mark 16:15).

Paul wasn't just waiting on some audible voice from God. He was taking the written Word of God and acting on it. But at the same time, he was in fellowship with the Lord. So, if God told Paul not to do something, he wouldn't do it.

In the dream, a man said, "*Come over into Macedonia, and help us*" (Acts 16:9). So, the next morning, Paul arose, believing that the Holy Spirit had called them into Macedonia and went over there. He had a direct word from the Lord, so we know this wasn't *his* dream.

This is what God told him to do. And yet, when he got into Philippi, he was only preaching the Word for a brief period before people came against him (Acts 16:22–24). They actually beat him and put him in a dungeon in the lowest part of the prison. And there he was with Silas, their hands and feet in the stocks.

Many people who found themselves in that situation may have said, "We missed God." But that wasn't the case for Paul and Silas. They were right in the center of God's will, and there was opposition against them. And at that point, where else were they going to go? They were committed!

Instead of griping and complaining, they started praising God at midnight. The Lord got to tapping His foot to their singing, and an earthquake came (Acts 16:25–32). It opened all the doors, their chains fell off, and they saw the prison keeper born again. It was just a tremendous time.

They could have been sitting there in prison, sucking their thumbs and thinking, *God, I thought we were obeying You. I thought You led us here. How come these bad things happened to us?* But they had already made a decision that they weren't going to quit. Because they knew God had called them there, they knew they were in His will. They could rejoice even when things looked bad because they had a relationship with God and trusted in the Lord.

'Get it Together!'

Years ago, a man picked me up in his private airplane and took me to cast a demon out of a girl. He was a brand-new pilot, and it was a tiny plane. It was so small that one of my shoulders was touching the window, the other shoulder was touching the pilot, and his shoulder was touching the other window.

On the way back, we ran into a storm over New Mexico. This guy hadn't earned his instrument rating yet, so he could only fly in visible conditions. And since he couldn't get above the storm in his little plane, we flew under it.

The wind was blowing that plane all over the place and this guy was having a hard time flying through the storm. He was screaming and praying in tongues, doing everything to keep that plane under control. Eventually, this guy just put his hands over his eyes, curled up in a fetal position, and yelled, "My God, we're going to die! We're going to die!"

I had to do something. So, I grabbed the yoke and just started flying that plane. For about an hour, I was steering that plane with one hand while I was shaking the pilot with the other and saying, "Get it together! God didn't let me live through Vietnam just so I could die in your plane!"

At one point, we flew over the White Sands Missile Range near Alamogordo, which is not something you're supposed to do in a private plane. Someone from the military came on our radio and said, "You're in restricted air space. We're going to shoot you out of the air if you don't turn around." So, I responded, "Don't shoot! The pilot is in a fetal position, and I've never flown an airplane before. Have mercy on me!"

After that, we never heard from them again. I imagine it's because they were laughing so hard that they couldn't speak! But we eventually got through that weather, buzzed the ground to scatter some cows, and landed in a pasture. I had Jamie come pick me up, and I never flew with that guy again!

You see, it's not like I could just start crying and get into a fetal position like this other guy. I had to keep trusting God and just fly that plane. I had just ministered the Gospel, so I knew I was in God's will. And I had no other place to go! So, I just let the spirit of might come on me.

When you're in communion with the Lord and get into a crisis situation, you just can't afford to panic or turn back. The devil will only fight against you if he thinks you're going to quit. Once he realizes you'll keep trusting God, he'll stop. And as long as you don't quit, you'll win!

Chapter 24

Press Toward the Mark

Brethren, I count not myself to have apprehended: but this *one thing* I do, *forgetting those things which are behind, and reaching forth unto those things which are before, I press toward the mark for the prize of the high calling of God in Christ Jesus.*

Philippians 3:13–14

I've seen people try to pastor a church or have a traveling ministry, but just in case those things don't work out, they find something else to fall back on. I just don't think that's the way to approach life or leadership. The Apostle Paul said that he forgot everything else and just pressed toward the mark.

Paul had a goal for his life. He knew what God had called him to do, and he wanted to win the prize. Unfortunately, most people just want to go with the flow and are content to be average. They don't want to experience any resistance.

To reach our God-given potential, we have to face resistance and keep moving forward. That's because God has something special for you and the enemy is going to try and do everything possible to keep you from it.

God's not going to call everybody to do what I do. But I can guarantee you, God will call you to do something that is beyond your ability. He will place you in a position of influence. And to complete what the Lord has called you to do is going to require something more than what you can do in your own strength.

For example, one of the things that I think people don't use enough of in leadership is the ministry of the Holy Spirit. The Bible says that Christians need to be building themselves up on their "*most holy faith, praying in the Holy Spirit*" (Jude 20).

When you pray in tongues, you are building yourself up (1 Cor. 14:4). You are strengthening yourself. It's just like flipping a switch and turning on a dynamo—the supernatural power of God. But it requires you to stop relying on your own strength. You have to be willing to receive strength from God that goes beyond just what you can see in the natural.

Paul thanked God that he prayed in tongues more than anyone he knew (1 Cor. 14:18). He went through all kinds of hardships and persecutions for the Gospel's sake, and yet he stayed encouraged, thankful, and kept praising God. Paul is probably one of the greatest men who ever walked the face of the earth, considering the things God did in his life.

If you can look at your life and explain your accomplishments according to your own ability, then I believe you've missed God's calling on your life. And if you're going to finish your race and not quit, you are going to have to draw on your relationship with Him. You need to have God's power working in you and through you. Because if your life isn't supernatural, it's superficial!

Fix Your Heart

> *They have prepared a net for my steps; my soul is bowed down: they have digged a pit before me, into the midst whereof they are fallen* themselves. *Selah. My heart is fixed, O God, my heart is fixed: I will sing and give praise.*
>
> Psalm 57:6–7

I hope you don't take what I'm about to say as being mean, but we've got a lot of wimpy leaders in the church today. They think that if they just minister the Gospel correctly, everybody ought to love them. And the first time somebody says something negative about them, or one of their big givers gets up, walks out, and quits the church, they just fall apart like a two-dollar suitcase. If you aren't being persecuted, it's because you aren't living godly (2 Tim. 3:12). There is going to be opposition, and you just have to make a decision that you are not going to quit.

David said, "*My heart is fixed.*" That means he prepared himself. He got himself established in his relationship with God. David determined he would not change his course. And like David, you just need to predetermine that you are going to serve the Lord and not quit. One of the ways Jamie and I did that was to just burn all of our bridges behind us.

You see, years ago, when we were struggling financially, I used to think that I could just go out and get a job if something happened to the ministry. I even remember having a dream where I quit the ministry and *joined the Air Force* to pay off all our debts! That's not something I would do in the natural, but this dream just seemed so real that I was actually relieved when I woke up.

I lay there in bed thinking, *That was just a dream. Thank You, Jesus, that I didn't join the Air Force!* But my wife Jamie was right there and said, "It wasn't so bad that you had to go join the Air Force." My heart started pounding as I thought, *Oh, God! It wasn't a dream!* But I found out later that I had been talking in my sleep, Jamie heard the whole thing, and she decided to have some fun with it.

But now, we need more than $12,000 every hour of every day just to keep the ministry going. With the launch of our Gospel Truth Network and our Charis campus expansion project, our income will likely have to double over the next few years to keep up with the ministry's growth.

And as it turns out, this has made it *easier* for me to stay with God and trust Him. Because at this point, there's no way I could quit the ministry and find another job just to pay the bills! The stakes are just so high right now that I actually don't worry about our finances at all. I have no choice but to keep moving forward and complete what God has called me to.

'Hold On!'

Back in the 1970s, I went to a conference at Calvary Cathedral in Fort Worth, Texas, where Bob Nichols was the pastor. I really appreciate Pastor Bob. He is a great friend of mine today. But back then, I had only met him once previously, and it was not a positive experience. That was the only contact I had with Pastor Bob before going to his church for the conference. I thought that if he ever heard my name again, he'd probably turn and run in the opposite direction!

All of the big-name ministers at the time were there, and they were prophesying to each other, getting all kinds of awesome words from the Lord. I remember sitting in that huge auditorium full of people, right in the middle of my row, about twenty seats in from the aisle. I felt so small and insignificant. During the song service, they said, "Go around and greet someone," but that whole time, I was thinking, *God, I need help. I need somebody to encourage me.*

Right about then, Pastor Bob somehow saw me in a crowd of two thousand people. He got off the platform and ran back to where I was in the middle of my row. Pastor Bob gently pushed his way through all of those people and just started hugging me. It wasn't one of those little charismatic side hugs, either. He wrapped his arms around me and wouldn't let go. Pastor Bob started saying, "Brother, I love you, and God loves you. Don't quit! Hold on!" He just held on and ministered to me. Then, he went back up to the front of the auditorium.

That encouraged me. It blessed me to think that this well-known man who was hosting this big conference had singled me out. He didn't have to do that. I took it as an expression of God's love, and it really ministered to me. He saw something in me that only God could see. I had this vision of touching the whole world with the Gospel, but here I was feeling small and insignificant. What Pastor Bob did lit a fire under me, and it kept me from quitting on that vision.

All these years later, through our television ministry and Charis Bible College, we are taking the Gospel farther and deeper than ever before. We have schools all around the world and billions of people can watch our programs at any time. As a matter of fact, Pastor Bob faithfully served on my board of directors for many years and had a front-row seat to watch what God has done through this ministry.

Principle IX

Handling Persecution and Criticism

Chapter 25

You Will Face Resistance

But thou hast fully known my doctrine, manner of life, purpose, faith, longsuffering, charity, patience, persecutions, afflictions, which came unto me at Antioch, at Iconium, at Lystra; what persecutions I endured: but out of them *all the Lord delivered me. Yea, and all that will live godly in Christ Jesus shall suffer persecution.*

2 Timothy 3:10–12

If you are in a place of influence and a position of leadership for the Lord, I can guarantee that Satan is going to fight against you. There is going to be opposition and criticism from people at work, family members, and even people at your church.

The way I cope with criticism is that I go back to my relationship with God because He wants to constantly build me up and encourage me. The Lord is not condemning me (Rom. 8:1). And if I have a good relationship with God, His acceptance will overwhelm the criticism of other people.

You see, when people speak against you, it's like having a teacup full of criticism. But then you go to God, and He overwhelms that criticism with a tsunami of His love. There's just no good way to compare those two things.

I had a man come up to me one time after I ministered, and he just started rebuking me. He was telling me how terrible I was and criticizing everything I said. Now, I'm not saying that I do everything right, but this guy was just letting me have it.

Right in the middle of him rebuking me, I just looked at him and asked, "Who died and made you God?" This guy stopped talking and gave me a confused look. I said, "You aren't God. Why should I care what you think about me?" Once he recovered, this guy said, "Well, you should." But I responded, "I don't! Compared to God, you're nobody!"

Back during the Covid pandemic in 2020, we had people from the city meet with us at Charis Bible College. They wanted to know how we were going to respond. But it was not a good meeting. Some of them were critical of me, and one guy even stood up and accused me of having no integrity. He just said terrible things about us, but I told him, "I've been criticized by people a lot more important than you. I don't really care that much what you think." That really offended this guy, but that's the way I deal with things.

There are people who would be shocked by what I said because they are so sensitive to what everybody else thinks. I'm not saying that I go out of my way to offend people. But as a godly leader, I am just not going to let criticism affect me in light of my relationship with the Lord.

Stay Encouraged

> *And David was greatly distressed; for the people spake of stoning him, because the soul of all the people was grieved, every man for his sons and for his daughters: but David encouraged himself in the Lord his God.*
>
> 1 Samuel 30:6

If you like criticism, something's wrong with you. This is not the way that God made us to be. The Lord made us for fellowship, and I think that every single person desires to be loved and appreciated. But if you're going to be a godly leader, you can't just let criticism dictate how you respond to things.

You can get to the place where your relationship with God is such an important part of your life that you don't care what other people think or say about you. That doesn't mean you like people rejecting or criticizing you, but those things are not going to keep you up at night.

When somebody attacks me, the way I deal with it is to go back to the Lord and I encourage myself in Him. Because if God is pleased with me, then I really don't care what someone else thinks.

David was anointed to be king at seventeen years old (1 Sam. 16:13-14) while Saul was still on the throne. And for the next thirteen years, it seemed like everything went wrong for David. At one point, when David and his army of 600 men were with the Philistines, they left the town of Ziklag unprotected (1 Sam. 30:1–5). That was where their families were staying.

Seeing an opening, the Amalekites attacked, burned the town, and took all their possessions, wives, and children. It looked like David and his men had lost everything—and they were even considering stoning him! It would have been easy for David to get discouraged. But David encouraged himself in the Lord by seeking wisdom and direction (1 Sam. 30:6-7). David asked, "*Shall I pursue after this troop? shall I overtake them?*" And the Lord said, "*Pursue: for thou shalt surely overtake* them, *and without fail recover* all" (1 Sam. 30:8).

In this battle, they took back all their wives and children, along with all their possessions and all the spoil of the Amalekites. They actually ended up with more than they had before and, within a couple of days, David became the king of Israel. What he had been believing for thirteen years came to pass in a matter of hours. This happened right after it seemed all was lost.

There are vicious things going on in this world. It doesn't matter if you're in government, business, or ministry. If you are a leader who is trying to serve the Lord, Satan is going to fight against you. And if you are easily discouraged, then you ultimately are going to fail. You just need to stay encouraged in the Lord and seek Him when everything seems to be against you. If your relationship with the Lord is lacking, you won't be able to withstand the pressure.

Don't Compromise

> *From that* time *many of his disciples went back, and walked no more with him. Then said Jesus unto the twelve, Will ye also go away?*
>
> John 6:66–67

I think one of the greatest moments in Jesus' life was when He had just fed the 5,000 (John 6:1–13). The people came to Jesus and wanted to make Him king (John 6:15), but He knew the only reason they were following Him was because He fed them.

Jesus' miracle filled their bellies, but they weren't really committed to Him. So, He started pushing back against them by saying, "You aren't seeking me for the right reasons" (John 6:26–27). They tried to get Jesus to do another miracle similar to when Moses caused manna, or bread, to come down out of Heaven. Jesus had just multiplied food, so they were tempting Him to do more.

Jesus responded by telling them He was the manna that came down from heaven (John 6:32–40). He told them, "*I am that bread of life*" (John 6:48). And the people got offended. They thought Jesus was talking about cannibalism!

Most leaders today have such a desire to be accepted and affirmed that if they said something that people misunderstood, they would fall all over themselves trying to apologize and explain things. But not Jesus. He went on to say, "*Except ye eat the flesh of the Son of man, and drink his blood, ye have no life in you*" (John 6:53). From a public relations standpoint, He made things worse. And because of that, nearly all the people left!

If Jesus was like many leaders today, He would have turned around to His twelve disciples and said, "I need a hug." But He didn't do that. Jesus asked, "*Will ye also go away?*" In other words, He told them, "There's the door. If you want to leave, then leave."

I think that revealed a sense of who Jesus really was. Jesus wanted people to accept Him, but He would not compromise who He was. And when people misunderstood Him, He didn't go out of His way to explain things.

Jesus did only what He saw His Father do (John 5:19) and said only what His Father said (John 12:49). He stayed encouraged through His relationship with His Father. And because of that, Jesus stood when everybody left Him.

In an average meeting, I may have 1,000–2,000 people there. And if I preached something so strong that everyone just got up and walked out, I could imagine the things that would be written about me. Some people might even say, "Well, his ministry's finished." But many more people than that left Jesus, and it didn't slow Him down a bit. Jesus didn't compromise who He was, and godly leaders should do the same.

Chapter 26

Get Rooted

And these are they likewise which are sown on stony ground; who, when they have heard the word, immediately receive it with gladness; and have no root in themselves, and so endure but for a time: afterward, when affliction or persecution ariseth for the word's sake, immediately they are offended.

Mark 4:16–17

In the Parable of the Sower (Mark 4:3–20), the second type of soil Jesus describes was stony and shallow, meaning roots wouldn't be able to go deep enough to sustain a plant. A seed that germinates in shallow earth will put all its energies into growth above ground because there is nowhere else for its growth to go. When the sun starts drying out the plant, the root system isn't there to sustain it, and it will wither and die.

In a similar way, someone who isn't rooted in the Word of God will wither and fall away when persecution or criticism comes. The Lord showed me this when we were being persecuted in the Baptist church early on in our ministry.

In the early 1970s, we would attend Kenneth Copeland's meetings in Fort Worth, Texas, once a month, and I'd get fired up about what I was learning about faith. So, I'd come back to my Baptist church, and I'd preach these things. For the first week or two, we would see people saved, delivered, and healed. We were seeing miracles happen and it was awesome!

Then, there'd be criticism, and the pastor would call me in to say, "You aren't preaching out of the quarterly and you aren't preaching Baptist doctrine." So, by the third or the fourth week, I'd be teaching the same things, but nothing would happen. Nobody was getting set free. People would even fall asleep when I was preaching.

Then I'd go back and hear Kenneth Copeland at the next meeting, and I'd get fired up again. I'd come back to my church, and for a week or two it would be good, and then the whole cycle repeated itself. It was so predictable that I actually got to anticipating it.

I prayed, "God, what's going on?" So, the Lord showed me that I didn't have root in myself (Mark 4:17). I was quoting Kenneth Copeland, but the Word was not getting into my heart as a seed and taking root. It wasn't *my* revelation.

From that time on, I've never had to quote somebody else. I may hear someone say something good, but I meditate on the Word until that truth becomes mine. It gets rooted in me so that persecution and criticism won't affect me. My relationship with God through His Word keeps me grounded.

As a godly leader, you need to put down roots, so you won't be easily moved by criticism. When you seek wisdom through God's Word, it eventually becomes your revelation. And you'll have confidence in what He's called you to do and how to do it.

Strike a Nerve

When people are offended, they don't bring any fruit to perfection. As in the case of the stony ground, the seed is sown and the Word begins to work, but ultimately, the seed doesn't produce the desired results. The desired result is the mature plant and the fruit that's produced from it.

If you get offended, you don't have to reject the seed of God's Word to stop it from producing in your life. You don't have to come out and say, "Well, I'm just going to quit serving the Lord." Simply being offended is enough to stop all progress.

It will make you lose your momentum. You'll lose your excitement, joy, and peace. Instead of leading people forward into what God has for them, you'll be spending your time licking your wounds and responding to criticism. You won't be producing fruit.

A godly leader has to be able to persevere beyond affliction and persecution. Notice, Mark 4:17 says that those negative things came for the Word's sake. Satan is sending persecution and criticism against you to stop the Word of God.

Actually, if you understand things properly, when you are being persecuted you can take it as a compliment. Most people may not look at things that way. But when you throw a rock into a pack of dogs, the one who yelps the loudest is the one who got hit. In other words, the negative reaction is evidence of your effectiveness.

I can stand to be persecuted, but I can't stand to be ineffective. If I'm preaching the Word of God, but people just ignore me, and it has no impact on them, that's a reflection on me. But if people get mad and react negatively because I'm sharing from the Word, that's because they got hit.

The Word of God will make an impact on people. But rather than come up to a higher level, admit that they're wrong, and change something, it's easier for some to drag others down to their level. That's what persecution is all about. And if you are a godly leader, you're going to have to expect resistance and persevere through it.

When people get convicted by what you're saying, they are faced with a choice. They either have to humble themselves and repent—which most people are very hesitant to do—or they come against you and persecute you.

Here's another way to look at this: If a witness has damaging testimony against a defendant, the defendant's lawyer will try to discredit the witness. The lawyer doesn't have to dispute the testimony if he can somehow show the jury that the witness is not a person of integrity. Even though the testimony might be accurate and condemning to the client, that lawyer will make it irrelevant if the witness is discredited.

That's what persecution is all about. People either have to admit that what you're saying is right and change their lives, or they have to discredit you.

Vengeance Is the Lord's

> *Dearly beloved, avenge not yourselves, but* rather *give place unto wrath: for it is written, Vengeance* is *mine; I will repay, saith the Lord.*
>
> Romans 12:19

Unfortunately, some of the strongest criticism I've faced over the years has come from within the church. It began in the Baptist church I was raised in and has continued over the years as our ministry has grown. It seems like there are negative articles published about me all of the time, and many of them are written by people who say they are Christians.

There were times I would have responded to those things. When I was younger, I was ready to fight at the drop of a hat, and I would have been the one to drop the hat! But like my friend Joe Nay told me, by doing that I would have won the argument and lost the race. I ended up getting to the place where I just trusted God to handle things and stayed focused on what He called me to do.

Years ago, I remember there was a minister who got up in front of their people and criticized my ministry. Among other things, they said I was "the slickest cult since Jim Jones" and encouraged people to burn my materials. For those of you who don't remember Jim Jones, he was a preacher who convinced his church to sell everything they owned, build a commune in the jungles of South America, and eventually commit mass suicide. So, that was quite an accusation to make!

I don't know exactly why they said those things, and I could have responded by defending myself, but I was just so secure in my relationship with God that I didn't give it any more thought. In fact, when this same minister sent out a letter requesting finances for a project, we sent them money. I just continued being a blessing to them.

About twenty years later, we just happened to be scheduled as guests on the same television show. In the green room, they told me how much they enjoyed my *Gospel Truth* program and loved our ministry. We ended up exchanging phone numbers, and since then, we've had meals together. It was just awesome how the Lord repaired our relationship.

That would not have happened if I hadn't let the Lord defend me. You can let God defend you instead of defending yourself. If your attitude is that you've always got to be right and correct every wrong, God can't defend you. You can either let God defend you or you can defend yourself. But I can guarantee, God will defend you better than you could.

Chapter 27

Take the High Road

Recompense to no man evil for evil. Provide things honest in the sight of all men.

Romans 12:17

Back in the late 1970s, when we were leading six Bible studies in three different states, there was a young man who had a radical conversion experience and was healed of cancer. He got really turned on to the Lord and was bold about sharing his testimony with others.

At one point, he fasted for forty-seven days. Once it was over, he had a heavy meal that included steak and fries. If you've ever fasted before, you know that's not a good idea. It can be dangerous. So, he ended up getting sick and dying. Well, this young man had been going around saying that if anything ever happened to him, I would raise him from the dead. Now, God didn't tell me that, and I didn't say that, but he did.

We had about four hundred people in these Bible studies, and they were all planning to go to the funeral to see what was going to happen. The service was in a little town that was about two hundred miles away from where we lived, so I spent the night before the funeral with this guy's cousins.

These people lived in such a remote area that they had a one-mile dirt driveway just to reach the main dirt road. After that, it took twenty miles to get to the paved road that led to town. In other words, they were out in the middle of nowhere.

When we got ready to go to the funeral, this man's great-aunt came and picked us up. She was crying inconsolably, and we thought it was because this boy had died. But when she got to the main road, instead of turning to go to town, she went in the opposite direction. At first, we thought she was just disoriented, but then she drove off the road, went into a pasture, and threw the car keys out the window. That's when I asked, "What are you doing?"

This woman's sister, who was the young man's grandmother, was a practicing witch—and she hated me! The grandmother blamed me for getting him to believe in healing and raising people from the dead. And she threatened to disinherit her sister if I was allowed to go to that funeral, taking away two or three sections of land at 640 acres per section. So, the great-aunt kidnapped me, and we missed the funeral.

The people who came to the funeral saw that I didn't show up. And I went from leading six Bible studies a week to nothing. Every one of them contacted me and said, "We don't want you to come back." They basically ran me out of town on a rail, and we left in disgrace. Nobody wanted our ministry anymore, and it was just a hard time.

Be Better, Not Bitter

What was I going to do? If I had defended myself and told everybody about the situation, that would've hurt the family. I knew the young man's parents and his siblings. Defending myself in that situation would've been self-serving. It just would've embarrassed them if I had gone public about what happened. So, I just chose not to say anything at all.

Five years later, I was sitting in my office in Manitou Springs, Colorado, and a pastor walked in with another man. This man had gone to the pastor because he was having some problems. That pastor was able to tell that he was dealing with bitterness and unforgiveness. So, he asked this man, "What's going on in your life?" And this man started talking about the funeral that I didn't show up to. It turns out this man was the brother of the boy who had died!

When I didn't show up at his funeral, it gave people the wrong impression. After all, that young man had gone with me to my meetings and shared his testimonies. And through that, we had grown close like family. So, it was no wonder people were hurt. And in the case of this young man's brother, it had made him bitter and affected the rest of his life.

You see, Satan cannot do anything to you without your consent and cooperation. If your life is all messed up, it's not because of what somebody else has done. Other people might have been used by the devil to hurt you, but you still have a choice as to whether you become bitter or better.

In this case, something happened that was out of my control. I probably could have done things differently, and I would never put myself in that position again. But at the time, we just decided it was best for the family if we didn't try to defend ourselves.

I understand that's contrary to the way most people would have handled things. They would have fallen all over themselves and tried to explain what happened in an attempt to maintain their position of leadership and influence. But I've learned over the years that God will defend me if I let Him. And He will exalt me in due time (1 Pet. 5:6).

There are thousands of websites and articles out there that have attacked me and my ministry. In the past, my staff has come to me with these things, and I've had to tell them that I don't want any of our resources being diverted toward fighting back. All our energy needs to be focused on what God has called us to do to take the Gospel deeper and farther, not on defending me or my reputation.

Let God Exalt You

> *Forbearing one another, and forgiving one another, if any man have a quarrel against any: even as Christ forgave you, so also* do *ye.*
>
> Colossians 3:13

That pastor had enough wisdom to say to the man, "You need to get this straight." So, he drove him five and a half hours, all the way to Manitou Springs. I just happened to be there that day, and he said, "You two need to work this out." Then he closed the door and walked away.

And the brother of that young man just began to vent on me. He said, "You didn't even show up! Why would you have done that?" Since I felt like enough time had passed, I told the man exactly what had happened. I told him about his grandmother, the great-aunt, the car, the keys, and everything else.

Immediately, the man said, "That sounds just like my grandmother. We are so sorry." This guy who, just a few minutes before, had been so angry and bitter toward me, completely changed his perspective. He just repented. And later, the Lord orchestrated a meeting with his parents, and our relationship was put back together.

If you don't defend yourself, God will defend you in a way that you never could. If I had gone to those parents after the funeral and told them what the grandmother had done, it would've done nothing but hurt them. It wouldn't have solved the situation. I just relied on my relationship with the Lord when hundreds of people had criticized and rejected me. And five years later, God resolved things.

There have been so many relationships through the years that the Lord has put back together when it seemed hopeless. And it's all because I put my relationship with God first. I trusted Him to vindicate me because I was taking a stand on His Word and doing the things He called me to do instead of doing what everybody else said I should have done.

There are going to be times as a leader when you will be maligned. People will say outrageous things about you. And some of the people you lead will walk away. If you want to be a godly leader, you have to rely on God to defend you against persecution and criticism.

Now, I'm not saying you just allow people to run over you, but the Lord has ways of exposing things (Luke 12:2–3). People will reap what they sow (Gal. 6:7). And if you let God work on your behalf, you'll come through the fire and not even smell like smoke (Dan. 3:27).

If you humble yourself under the mighty hand of God, He will exalt you (1 Pet 5:6). You need to get to a place where it's all about the Lord, and if people don't like you and criticize you, it doesn't matter. It's just not a big deal.

Principle X

Delegate Authority

Chapter 28

Don't Do It All

And the things that thou hast heard of me among many witnesses, the same commit thou to faithful men, who shall be able to teach others also.

2 Timothy 2:2

If you're really going to be a godly leader, you need to learn how to delegate things to other people. And this goes back to a person's relationship with God. Someone who is insecure and feels like all of the responsibility is on them isn't looking to the Lord for guidance. They are trying to make everything happen on their own. People like that don't delegate things well because they don't think anybody can do it as well as they can.

Delegation is not something that you just automatically obtain. I pastored three little churches back in the 1970s, and one of my biggest failures was my inability to delegate. I was on fire for God. I had faith working in me. And when it came to praying for and ministering to people, I just believed I could do it better than most of the people in my church. I was afraid that if I called people forward for healing and let somebody else pray for them, they may not do it as well as I did. So, I didn't delegate anything.

That's one of the reasons that a lot of churches remain small. It's because many ministers think, *Nobody is as anointed as I am. Nobody can do it as well as I can.* But a single person can only effectively deal with so many people.

It's said that about 80 percent of churches in the United States have fewer than two hundred people.[11] That's because of a failure of leadership to delegate. People just want to do everything. They are perfectionists. They are refusing to turn things over because they are afraid someone will make a mistake. If God had that same attitude, none of us would be in ministry. That's because every one of us makes mistakes.

The way our ministry works, we've got over 1,200 employees, and I only oversee a team of five people. Each one of them oversees their own team, and those teams do the different things that make the ministry run. At the time of this writing, there are more than 160 different teams in our ministry. So, there's a leadership structure in place that helps us get things done.

I'm amazed at how the Lord has committed things to us. He's given us such leeway that we can make mistakes, and yet He doesn't pull back His calling (Rom. 11:29). But if you think you are indispensable to God's plan, just remember that the Lord has never had anybody qualified working for Him yet!

Find Quality People

You do need to identify people of quality before you delegate things. But if you have a strong personal relationship with God, He will bring people to you. I am thankful for all the people who have left successful careers and sold their homes just to join this ministry and help bring into reality the vision God gave me.

I remember back in 2002 when the Lord told me that I was limiting Him by my small thinking (Ps. 78:41), I just decided I was going to dream big. At that time, we only had twenty-five employees, and we were struggling because we couldn't find a manager who was a good fit.

Everyone we considered to manage the ministry were all Christians and loved the Lord, but some of them had never heard of me before they came to work for the ministry. They may have had some business sense or something else, but they had no connection with me. They just didn't understand the heart of this ministry.

For two years, we had been asking God to send us somebody who would serve as manager and help us grow. We wanted to delegate, but we just hadn't found the right person. So, I told the Lord, "I'm going to go for it. And You're going to have to bring me the people to help us grow. We are doing the maximum that we can do right now."

At about that time, I had a death in my family. I had to call my board of directors and tell them that we were going to cancel an upcoming board meeting. One of my board members worked for a large retail business, and he trained all of the managers in a high-visibility part of the organization. When I called to cancel the board meeting, this man said, "I'm glad you called because God has spoken to me. I'm taking early retirement, and I'm coming out there to take your ministry to the next level."

When he said those things, I was just overwhelmed. I was thinking, *God, I didn't even ask this guy to come help us. You just sent him to me.* And that person was with us for a long time as we grew from twenty-five to 350 employees.

On the other hand, there was a man who led a major worldwide ministry with over a thousand employees. He picked people to serve on his board who were experts and successful at business, but who just didn't have the same heart as him. In the end, this board forced the man out of the ministry he founded and built from the ground up. And it was all because they didn't have the right heart for the ministry and put other priorities first.

The Right Heart

We spend a lot of time in our ministry casting the vision and trying to tell our staff what's happening because it takes every single one of them to make things work. From the people who clean the toilets, to the people who make the food, to the people who serve in the children's ministry during our events, every single person is vital to our success. So, we've got to keep the vision in front of them. That way, they are all serving with the same heart.

We have thousands of people helping Jamie and me do what we used to do all by ourselves. For our ministry to grow and complete the vision God has for us, we've had to trust other people and bring them in to help us. And it has just been amazing.

People will make mistakes, but that doesn't mean you shouldn't delegate things. You cannot micromanage everything as a leader. We had one guy in our ministry leadership who did a lot of great things for us, but at the same time, he was keeping count of how many pencils and notebooks everyone was using. That was not a good use of his time or authority.

I've had similar conversations with other people we've promoted. I had to tell them that they just cannot counsel every single person or personally address every single issue. They have to come up to a 30,000-foot view of things and delegate the management of other tasks to their teams.

Also, you may delegate to people who turn around and hurt you. Years ago, we had one person in leadership whose actions could have destroyed the ministry. On paper, this person looked like they would be awesome. Before they came to us, this person oversaw a whole region of the world for their former employer, managing thousands of people. Still, I just didn't feel right about them.

This person kept getting promoted and made it to a high level of leadership in the ministry. But at the same time, they were doing destructive things behind the scenes, like contacting our partners and telling people I was leading a cult.

Thankfully, one of our employees exposed this person for what they were doing, and we were able to deal with it. This employee put his own career on the line by speaking up, but he did so because he actually had a heart for the ministry. As a result, he's since been promoted through the ranks to a position of major leadership.

Delegating to the wrong person could have caused a lot of damage, but because I have a relationship with the Lord, He just took care of it. Even if you make a mistake, God can fix it. The Lord can bring the right people to you who will help you accomplish what He's called you to do.

Chapter 29

They Will Be Sent

And the word of the Lord came unto [Elijah], *saying, Get thee hence, and turn thee eastward, and hide thyself by the brook Cherith, that* is *before Jordan. And it shall be,* that *thou shalt drink of the brook; and I have commanded the ravens to feed thee there.*

1 Kings 17:2–4

There's a man who's been overseeing the construction of our Charis Bible College student housing in recent years who was sent to us by God. There's just no other way to explain it.

This man had been involved in major building projects for years in the secular world. He helped build professional sports stadiums and arenas in several large cities. He was even part of building the Sphere in Las Vegas, which cost $2.3 billion.[12] So, he already had quite a track record.

A few years ago, we had a partner banquet at one of our events and our CEO Billy Epperhart got to talking to this man. As it turned out, he had been a partner with the ministry for a long time. So, this guy just left everything behind and came to work for us.

This man's testimony was that he received a word from the Lord twenty years before. God told him that he would construct buildings "here and there." At the time, this man was working on a project in Jacksonville, Florida. That was the "here" the Lord spoke about. Then, years later, when this man and his wife first came to Woodland Park to check out our Charis campus, he drove past our main gate and saw our sign that says, "Welcome to your place called 'there.'"

We put up that sign to remind our students of the story of the Prophet Elijah, who was called to certain places where the Lord would provide for him (1 Kgs. 17:2–4). Many times, people make excuses about why they can't attend Charis, but they'll find that God will provide everything they need when they get "there."

In this case, this man and his wife took it as confirmation that they were doing the right thing in coming to Colorado to help us. And that's just one way the Lord showed that He was sending the right person to us and that we could delegate things to him.

This man had shown he had a heart for the ministry by being a partner. He was also seeking the Lord about where he should be. Here was a guy who built things worth billions of dollars that are seen by millions of people in person and on television, and I didn't ask God to send Him. The Lord just led him to us. I'm sure he had many other opportunities that were lucrative and high visibility, but he followed the leading of the Lord.

Where Their Treasure Is

For where your treasure is, there will your heart be also.

Matthew 6:21

Many times, because of insecurity, a person will hire someone who's exactly like them. They don't want anybody around them who may have a different approach toward things because they get intimidated by it. That goes back to a lack of security in our relationship with God and trusting that He has the best people in mind to help you.

If all you do is hire people who are exactly like you, then you have doubled your strengths and doubled your weaknesses. You need people who are different than you, and yet they need to have your heart. One way to determine whether someone has your heart is by observing where they put their money.

For example, if you are in business, and the person you're considering for a position never tried your product or service, it's unlikely they are going to be as passionate about your vision as you are. That's why some companies offer product discounts to employees to encourage their loyalty.

In ministry, a leader can learn about someone through their giving. Charlie and Jill LeBlanc led worship at our events for years. But before the Lord brought them to us, they were connected with another major media ministry.

Years ago, Charlie and Jill started out on their own, ministering at small churches. But once they got the revelation that gifts could make room for them in front of people of influence (Prov. 18:16), they felt led to give to a much larger ministry.

It wasn't long before that ministry invited Charlie and Jill to lead worship at their events. They suddenly went from ministering in small venues to traveling the world for several years and seeing tens of thousands of people come to those meetings.

The lead minister told them, "I thought about you doing praise and worship for us, but the first thing I did was go check your giving to see if you were partners with us." Their consistent giving showed that they could be trusted with a huge responsibility.

Another way to identify someone is through faithfulness. Our friend, Pastor Bob Yandian, led Grace Fellowship in Tulsa, Oklahoma, for many years. He had a bookstore in the church to provide resources to his people, but no matter who he put in charge over it, the business struggled.

One day, he was at his church and saw a woman cleaning the seats in the sanctuary and praying over each one as she went. In that moment, the Lord spoke to Bob and said, "You're looking for qualified people, but you need to look for faithful people." God showed him that a person can be trained to develop skills, but faithfulness isn't something that can be taught.

He ended up hiring this woman who was a housewife and never worked a job before and put her over the bookstore. And for years after that, the bookstore was successful because the person with the right heart was put in the right place.

Some Assembly Required

> *And let us consider one another to provoke unto love and to good works: Not forsaking the assembling of ourselves together, as the manner of some* is; *but exhorting* one another*: and so much the more, as ye see the day approaching.*
>
> Hebrews 10:24–25

The thing that blesses me so much when I see the Lord bringing people who will help the ministry is that it's a demonstration of the Body of Christ at work.

Years ago, when Daniel Amstutz came on staff at Charis as worship leader, he asked me, "Well, what do you want me to do?" And I said, "You're the one who's anointed to do praise and worship. You don't tell me what to preach, and I won't tell you what to sing."

That's one of the things that makes a good ministry work. God brings people together who are already anointed instead of just letting one person try to do everything. I can't do the work of people who are anointed to create stage plays, produce television programs, and lead praise and worship. God just brings people to us who know how to do these things.

For example, I held meetings at Pastor Greg Mohr's church in Decatur, Texas, for about twenty years. He had an awesome church, but he felt led to join our ministry. Pastor Greg came to me and said, "I love being here and I love what I'm doing—and if you tell me differently, I'll stay where I am for the rest of my life and never complain—but I really feel called to work at Charis."

Since then, he's been involved with Charis Bible College, our World Outreach ministry, Charis Alumni, the third-year Ministry School, and the Association of Related Ministries International. It's just awesome to see God assembling different callings and ministries together. It's what has allowed us to have the kind of impact we've had.

A few years ago, when I was ministering at Pastor Duane Sheriff's Victory Life Church, I held up a 9 mm bullet and asked the crowd, "Who's afraid of this?" Then I said, "If I threw this bullet and hit somebody, it might make a little ding, but it's not going to kill you." Since it was just a bullet, nobody was afraid of it.

Then, Pastor Duane came up with a box full of parts and assembled a pistol while I was speaking. Once all the pieces were put together and the bullet was loaded, then it was totally different. All the elements to create something powerful were already there, but they weren't assembled.

It's the same with people, especially the Body of Christ. There is a difference between just being in an organization together and being assembled together—where every part is doing what they are called to do. As a godly leader, when you delegate authority to anointed people, you are helping them find their place and making your organization more powerful.

Chapter 30

Let Others Help You

When Jamie and I met with Oral Roberts in 2009, he prayed over us and something just exploded on the inside of me. Throughout his life, Oral had ministered healing to millions of people, built a university, been a pioneer in media ministry, and did so many other things. I'll tell you, when you get around a visionary and godly leader like that, it just rubs off on you!

That's when I realized I was limiting God again, and I needed to start thinking bigger. At the time, we were contemplating the next steps for our Bible college. Just a few years earlier, we had moved from a 14,600-square-foot facility to a space that had 110,000 square feet—and we had quickly outgrown it! We considered a number of options, including capping enrollment, splitting the classes across multiple sites, or finding property to build on.

I prayed about it, and the Lord said, "This is bigger than what you can do on your own. You've got to have people help you accomplish it." Then, He showed me five of the leaders within our ministry and told me to submit my vision to them.

That was a scary proposition. As I've said, I'd been wary about sharing what God's shown me with other people. It's kind of like petting a dog. If every time you reached out your hand, he bit you, pretty soon you'd stop trying to pet him.

That's how I was about sharing my vision. To some degree, I had overcome that back in 2002 when the Lord first showed me that I was limiting Him through my small thinking. But I still had reservations about sharing things with my leadership and delegating to them. One of the men who was a leader in our ministry seemed like he was always keeping his foot on the brake. He often thought I was dreaming too big. So, I just wasn't going to share these things unless the Lord told me to do it.

I ended up going in and telling these guys what God was putting on my heart, and I did it in fear and trembling. I was taking what the Lord had been speaking to me all those years, and I was just putting it before them for their consideration. But instead of just saying, "No, you're dreaming too big," they all rose to the occasion. One of them even suggested we look at a piece of property in Woodland Park.

As it turned out, once we all went there and looked at what would become the home of our main campus, every one of them eventually agreed that we should go for it. But that only happened because I was obedient to the Lord and delegated something to other men who had a heart for our ministry and grabbed hold of the vision together with me. I've learned that if your vision isn't big enough to require help from someone else, it likely isn't from God.

Be Willing to Let Go

Happy and Jeanne Caldwell are friends of mine. They pastored Agape Church in Little Rock, Arkansas, for thirty-five years. They founded it, helped it grow, and built millions of dollars' worth of facilities. And yet, when God said that He had a new assignment for Happy, he turned the church over to another minister.

In a sense, this is about the highest degree of delegation you can reach. Here was someone who had been in leadership for decades, and he just gave it all away at the Lord's direction. Happy walked away from that church and started over. That's a person who has a strong relationship with God.

Most people think the American dream is to get all you can, can all you get, and then sit on your can. They think their accomplishments and material wealth just belong to them because they worked for it. But Happy Caldwell looked at everything as God's. He saw himself as a steward. So, when God told Happy there was another assignment for him, he was willing to move on.

I was at a minister's conference where Happy shared all this. He talked about the transition from the church into his new assignment, and then he challenged people. Happy asked us, "Have you ever considered that maybe God wants you to turn your ministry over, and that He's got something else for you?" Then he said, "I want you to pray and ask the Lord if you are doing what He wants you to do."

It didn't take me long before I told God, "If You want me to turn my ministry over to somebody else and start all over, I'll do it." In saying that, I was making sure that I was walking humbly with the Lord (Mic. 6:8) and being dependent upon Him.

Even though this ministry is growing exponentially, and we are touching people all over the world with the Gospel, I can honestly say that I could walk away and just do whatever God told me to do. I'd even live in a grass hut in Africa if that's what He called me to do. Now, Jamie has told me that I might have to go to Africa by myself if that's the case! But if the Lord told me to walk away from everything, I'd do it. I think that's a sign of godly leadership.

After all these years in ministry and leadership, I recognize that I am just a steward of what God has given me. The Lord is doing some miraculous things right now, but I am also thinking about legacy and succession. Everyone has an expiration date, including me. And at some point, I will have to turn these things over to someone else.

Plan for Succession

> *Let the Lord, the God of the spirits of all flesh, set a man over the congregation, which may go out before them, and which may go in before them, and which may lead them out, and which may bring them in; that the congregation of the Lord be not as sheep which have no shepherd.*
>
> Numbers 27:16–17

Moses spoke these things as he was looking at the end of his own life and considering who would lead the children of Israel into the Promised Land. In response, the Lord chose Joshua, "*a man in whom is the spirit*"—someone with the right heart—to be his successor (Num. 27:18).

In 2017, the Lord spoke to me about a succession plan. And as Jamie and I were praying about it, Mike and Carrie Pickett just kept coming up. We realized they had the right heart for the ministry and were the right people to take everything to the next level. So, they spent the next few years receiving guidance from Jamie and me, along with training from our CEO Billy Epperhart.

During that process, Mike and Carrie came to us and said, "If at any time, God leads you to choose someone else to do this, we'll submit to that." That's a humble attitude! They put the ministry before any benefit they would receive for themselves. And it just confirmed what the Lord had already been showing us. So, in 2024, we announced that we would pass the baton of leadership to Mike and Carrie.

Now, I'm not planning on going anywhere. I'm going to continue doing what the Lord has called me to do all these years. But this was just an opportunity to fulfill what the Apostle Paul said about committing the truths God revealed to me to faithful people "who shall be able to teach others also" (2 Tim. 2:2).

Since we made that announcement, I've heard about other ministries who are considering coming up with their own succession plans. I don't think it was any special wisdom on my part. It's just evidence of my relationship with the Lord and part of being a godly leader.

Even now, as I continue to grow, I'm still learning how to become a better leader. And I'm doing everything to the best of my abilities to train up other leaders who will serve God. I believe we'll do even more things and reach even more people with the nearly-too-good-to-be-true message of the Gospel than ever before. And I believe the best is yet to come!

Conclusion

It's been said that if you try to lead people and nobody follows, you're just out for a walk. Sad to say, so many people are out in the world saying they are leaders, but no one is actually following.

That's why you see people going to conferences and reading books, trying to find some nugget of wisdom on how to be a leader. In many cases, they are just trying to promote themselves and look important. The truth is, if they'd just focus on their relationship with God, they would grow into a position of influence.

I hope that as you read this book, you've not only seen how to become a godly leader but also how to develop your relationship with the Lord. The things I've shared are really just different dynamics of having a personal relationship with God.

If you are truly seeking a relationship with the Lord, you'll humble yourself. If you recognize that God is God, and you are not, you will develop character and integrity. When you free yourself from distractions and spend time with God, you will hear Him. When you decide you won't compromise on God's Word, He'll reveal His vision to you. An anointing will come to help you fulfill what God has shown you. Patience will develop as you manifest the presence of God in your life. As you learn to endure hardness, you'll be less likely to quit. After you commit to finishing your course, you'll be able to handle persecution and criticism. And as you become secure in God's opinion of you, the things to which He's called you can be delegated to others.

As I said at the beginning, I didn't seek these things about leadership. They've just come to me as I've grown in my relationship with God. I've always made that the focus of my life. And everything has flowed from that.

A few years ago, our friend John Donnelly shared a word with me. John said the Lord would give me the same opportunity that He gave Solomon—that whatever I asked for, He would grant it (2 Chr. 1:7). Solomon responded that he needed the Lord's help as he took the throne of his father, King David (2 Chr. 1:8–9). He asked for wisdom and understanding to be a just ruler and leader of God's people (2 Chr. 1:10).

I realize that, like Solomon, I could have asked for anything, including wisdom and understanding. But as I prayed about it, the thing that kept coming back to me was, "I just want to know you more, Lord." So, I told the Lord that was what I wanted more than anything. I just want to know Him more. I believe that's how I've lived my entire life, and that's what has allowed me to lead people in a godly way.

If you'll focus on your relationship with God, He will promote you. And if you trust the Lord and keep growing in that relationship, all of these other things will fall into place. You will truly be a *godly* leader.

Receive Jesus as Your Savior

Choosing to receive Jesus Christ as your Lord and Savior is the most important decision you'll ever make!

God's Word promises, *"That if thou shalt confess with thy mouth the Lord Jesus, and shalt believe in thine heart that God hath raised him from the dead, thou shalt be saved. For with the heart man believeth unto righteousness; and with the mouth confession is made unto salvation"* (Rom. 10:9–10). *"For whosoever shall call upon the name of the Lord shall be saved"* (Rom. 10:13). By His grace, God has already done everything to provide salvation. Your part is simply to believe and receive.

Pray out loud: "Jesus, I acknowledge that I've sinned and need to receive what you did for the forgiveness of my sins. I confess that You are my Lord and Savior. I believe in my heart that God raised You from the dead. By faith in Your Word, I receive salvation now. Thank You for saving me."

The very moment you commit your life to Jesus Christ, the truth of His Word instantly comes to pass in your spirit. Now that you're born again, there's a brand-new you!

Please contact us and let us know that you've prayed to receive Jesus as your Savior. We'd like to send you some free materials to help you on your new journey. Call our Helpline: **719-635-1111** (available 24 hours a day, seven days a week) to speak to a staff member who is here to help you understand and grow in your new relationship with the Lord.

Welcome to your new life!

Receive the Holy Spirit

As His child, your loving heavenly Father wants to give you the supernatural power you need to live a new life. *"For every one that asketh receiveth; and he that seeketh findeth; and to him that knocketh it shall be opened...how much more shall* your *heavenly Father give the Holy Spirit to them that ask him?"* (Luke 11:10–13).

All you have to do is ask, believe, and receive! Pray this: "Father, I recognize my need for Your power to live a new life. Please fill me with Your Holy Spirit. By faith, I receive it right now. Thank You for baptizing me. Holy Spirit, You are welcome in my life."

Some syllables from a language you don't recognize will rise up from your heart to your mouth (1 Cor. 14:14). As you speak them out loud by faith, you're releasing God's power from within and building yourself up in the spirit (1 Cor. 14:4). You can do this whenever and wherever you like.

It doesn't really matter whether you felt anything or not when you prayed to receive the Lord and His Spirit. If you believed in your heart that you received, then God's Word promises you did. *"Therefore I say unto you, What things soever ye desire, when ye pray, believe that ye receive* them, *and ye shall have* them*"* (Mark 11:24). God always honors His Word—believe it!

We would like to rejoice with you, pray with you, and answer any questions to help you understand more fully what has taken place in your life!

Please contact us to let us know that you've prayed to be filled with the Holy Spirit and to request the book *The New You & the Holy Spirit.* This book will explain in more detail about the benefits of being filled with the Holy Spirit and speaking in tongues. Call our Helpline: **719-635-1111** (available 24 hours a day, seven days a week).

Notes

1. Eric Metaxas, "Eric Liddell," August 9, 2024, https://ericmetaxas.com/watch-read/blog/eric-liddell-and-the-1924-paris-olympics/

2. Greg McKevitt, "'It's Complete Surrender': Olympics Hero Eric Liddell and the True Story Behind Chariots of Fire," BBC, July 8, 2024, https://www.bbc.com/culture/article/20240705-olympics-hero-eric-liddell-and-the-real-story-behind-chariots-of-fire

3. *Blue Letter Bible*, s.v. "רַק" ("raq"), accessed December 12, 2024, https://www.blueletterbible.org/lexicon/h7535/kjv/wlc/0-1/

4. Savannah Barry, "Duty is ours, results are God's," Patriot Academy, accessed December 12, 2024, https://www.patriotacademy.com/duty-is-ours-results-are-gods/

5. "Black Mirror or Black Hole? American Phone Screen Time Statistics," Harmony Healthcare IT, January 8, 2024, https://www.harmonyhit.com/phone-screen-time-statistics

6. *Blue Letter Bible*, s.v. "יָדַע" ("yâda'"), accessed December 12, 2024, https://www.blueletterbible.org/lexicon/h3045/kjv/wlc/0-1/

7. *Strong's Definitions*, s.v. "יֵצֶר" ("yēṣer"), accessed December 13, 2024, https://www.blueletterbible.org/lexicon/h3336/kjv/wlc/0-1/

8. *Blue Letter Bible*, s.v. "kûn" ("כּוּן"), accessed January 6, 2025, https://www.blueletterbible.org/lexicon/h3559/kjv/wlc/0-1/

9. Trisha R. Peach, "Burnout, Timeout, and Fallout: A Qualitative Study of Why Pastors Leave Ministry," (Doctoral thesis, Bethel University, 2022), 7, 49-50, and 134, https://spark.bethel.edu/etd/805

10. James Dobson, "Pastors And Churches Are Struggling," *Apostolic Information Service*, Dec. 20, 2007, https://www.apostolic.edu/pastors-and-churches-are-struggling/

11. Charita Goshay, "'Difficult Days Are Ahead' for America's Churches, Faith Institutions," Akron Beacon Journal, August 22, 2020, https://www.beaconjournal.com/story/news/local/2020/08/22/lsquodifficult-days-are-aheadrsquo-for-americarsquos-churches-faith-institutions/42282593/

12. Rebecca Heilweil, "The Sphere Is Here. Are We Ready for More High-Tech Architecture?," *Smithsonian Magazine*, October 16, 2023, https://www.smithsonianmag.com/innovation/the-sphere-is-here-are-we-ready-for-more-high-tech-architecture-180983077/

Call for Prayer

If you need prayer for any reason, you can call our Helpline, 24 hours a day, seven days a week at **719-635-1111**. A trained prayer minister will answer your call and pray with you.

Every day, we receive testimonies of healings and other miracles from our Helpline, and we are ministering God's nearly-too-good-to-be-true message of the Gospel to more people than ever. So, I encourage you to call today!

About the Author

Andrew Wommack's life was forever changed the moment he encountered the supernatural love of God on March 23, 1968. As a renowned Bible teacher and author, Andrew has made it his mission to change the way the world sees God.

Andrew's vision is to go as far and deep with the Gospel as possible. His message goes far through the *Gospel Truth* television program, which is available to over half the world's population. The message goes deep through discipleship at Charis Bible College, headquartered in Woodland Park, Colorado. Founded in 1994, Charis has campuses across the United States and around the globe.

Andrew also has an extensive library of teaching materials in print, audio, and video. More than 200,000 hours of free teachings can be accessed at **awmi.net**.

There's more on the website!

Discover FREE teachings, testimonies, and more by scanning the QR code.

Continue to grow in the Word of God! You'll be blessed!

Your monthly giving makes the greatest kingdom impact.

When you give, you make an impact in the kingdom that lasts for generations. Your generosity enables our phone ministers to answer calls 24/7. Your support is also expanding Charis Bible College and allowing *The Gospel Truth* to reach an even wider global audience. You do this and more through your giving each month!

Become a Grace Partner today!
Scan the QR code or call our Helpline at 719-635-1111 and select option five for Partnership.